MW00640646

These birds are the worst.

A Dumb Birds
Field Guide to the
WORST BIRDS EVER

Matt Kracht

CHRONICLE BOOKS
San Francisco

Copyright © 2025 by Matthew Kracht.

All rights reserved. No part of this book may be reproduced in any
form without written permission from the publisher.

Library of Congress Cataloging-in-Publication
Data available.

ISBN 978-1-7972-3275-1

Manufactured in China.

Design by Maggie Edelman and Liz Li.

Chronicle Books LLC
680 Second Street
San Francisco, CA 94107

www.chroniclebooks.com

10 9 8 7 6 5 4 3 2 1

For *Herr Professor Dr. Jerry Kracht*, who has always been and continues to be my model for love, good humor, and generosity of spirit. Thanks, Dad, for instilling in me the joy of the arts and an appreciation for a well-crafted dirty limerick, and for teaching me that German humor is no laughing matter.

Contents

Introduction

Today I took a long walk outdoors.

I do this regularly because my doctor insisted—he said that walking outdoors is "good for the nerves," and also that it might help put me in "a calmer and more centered state of mind."

Naturally, I pointed out to him that *everyone* knows a little fresh air and exercise is good for you, but did he know that many *experts* believe that the meditative nature of walking can help unlock potential in art, writing, and other intellectual pursuits that require mental focus and creativity? To which my doctor got rather snippy about which one of us went to medical school.

I noted his apparent irritability and mentioned that he might reconsider which one of us should be taking walks for their nerves. He did not seem to appreciate my suggestion.

Anyway, during the course of today's walk, I was startled by starlings, flapped at by finches, jabbered at by juncos, and swooped, scolded, and snubbed by scrub jays. I won't even bring up what the goddamn crows perpetrated.

This sort of abuse is not unusual for me. I find that personal harassment by birds is a near-daily occurrence, so I have more or less given up on the idea of any calm, meditative reflection or mindful awareness happening while I'm outdoors. Thanks to birds, I'm forced to settle for mere physical exercise from my walks.

I suppose that should be enough, but it sort of feels like a rip-off when everyone else out for a stroll seems to be attaining blissful states of centered consciousness, having flashes of inspiration, and enjoying sudden creative breakthroughs on the novels they're all writing.

But not me. Even when I'm not being actively hassled by birds, how could I relax with those feathered bastards lurking in the trees? They're like gangs of juvenile delinquents hanging around street corners, just killing time until their next mugging victim walks by.

Now, you might be wondering, "What is the point?"

Believe me, I ask myself this question daily.

But in this particular case, the point is that *birds suck*—not only that, but many of them are incredibly stupid. Some are even more stupid than finches, which, I think we can all agree, is really saying something.

However, beyond this general avian suckage, there are some birds who are truly substandard, even for birds. Birds whose personal style and taste are so abominable, whose sense of civility is so bankrupt, and whose behavior is so irritating that it staggers the imagination!

Therefore, in spite of my ongoing persecution by the local birds, not to mention a certain doctor's constant admonitions to "just drop it," I intend to pursue my ongoing study of avians at large, and continue to document their names, behaviors, and individual criminal offenses.

Some might call this an obsession, but I think of it as more of a moral duty.

That said, I recently decided that I needed to pause in my mission, at least long enough to call out a number of birds that *really* make my head ache, which is why I've authored this book.

You may be thinking, "We're all aware of your advanced studies in the field of Bird Criticism. In fact, didn't you already write a book about this?"

Two. It's actually *two* books, since you brought it up (both bestsellers, I might add).

But never mind that—in *this* book I am excited to finally share with the public some exciting new bird science (developed by me), and to use my new, cutting-edge analytical methods to call out those species that I believe are the most egregious transgressors against courtesy, decorum, and public tranquility.

"Yes, yes," you may be thinking, "of course birds are terrible. Everyone knows that. But honestly, can't you just let it go and get on with your life?"

Fair question. Allow me to elaborate my position:

Ha ha, NO! I can't let it go! Have you been listening to me at all? Birds are TERRIBLE. I have spent years, YEARS, of my life studying birds. Watching them. Analyzing their behaviors. Determining their "contributions" to the world. I am an expert, so believe me when I tell you this: Birds are horrible people.

And the birds included in THIS book are, by far, the worst of the lot. Of all the shit-eating birds that I've had the misfortune to catalog over the course of my career as a scientist and professional bird critic, THESE birds take the fucking SHIT-CAKE!

Sorry. I'm sorry. I get worked up.

Deep breaths.

Just like the doctor said, "In through the nose, out through the mouth. And for god's sake, man, try to unclench your body or you're going to rupture something."

Anyway, as I was saying, these birds are definitely the worst. You've been warned.

Said that poetry could be a "healthy way to explore emotions surrounding birds + bird-related incidents"— Dr. M. went on and on about how the Journal of the American Medical Assn. recently put some poetry in their precious pages. Apparently it's now considered a "healing tool." (Told M. who the healing tool was, but agreed to give it a try anyway.)

HAIKUS

Little brownish bird
full of chattering blather
why won't you shut up?

~~Duck~~ ~~Ducky~~ floats on water
Quacking to no one at all
You eat too much bread.

Strutting like a king
Honk honk honk honk honk honk ~~Whonk~~ honk
Go fuck yourself, goose

~~healing tool~~

a passerine called the great tit
has birdwatchers all in a snit
the name sounds "risqué"
but sorry to say
they just perch in trees and take shits!

This is a snide one

How to Use This Book

Whether you are an avid bird-watcher or new to the endeavor, you may benefit from familiarizing yourself with this guide and its different parts, especially the part with the birds in it.

Each entry includes an illustration, a description, and corresponding notes on a bird's range, behavior, calls, and what the hell the bird's problem is. These are intended not only to aid with proper identification, but also to help you on your way to a deeper understanding of their personality flaws.

You will also find sections in this book on a number of related topics, including where to observe birds, methods of identification, bird anatomy, and some useful strategies for emotional self-care. (If you are new to birding, that last one might seem out of place, but you will thank me for it later.)

Where to Look for Birds

Here's the deal: Birds are kind of everywhere. If you're not finding any, it might help to adjust your routine. For example, try putting your phone down and going outside once in a while. While you're out there, try looking around you. You can't help but eventually see a bird.

Not sure where to start? That's okay, some people just need a lot of hand-holding. Here are a few ideas for where to look. If you study these places with any effort at all, you should start to notice that they are full of birds:

1. **Obviously, out in nature.** Nature is infested with birds. If you don't immediately spot one in the air, you can also find birds in trees, in bushes, floating in water, and possibly even just standing around on the ground. If you don't see them at first, try listening, because nearby birds will likely be heard messing up the peaceful nature vibes with their incessant chatter.

2. **In your garden.** If you have even a modest garden or a few trees outside your home, try looking there—birds are too dumb to know the difference between a garden and nature. If you don't have a garden, your neighbor might. Ask them before going into it, and remember, you have no idea who stepped on those flowers.

3. **In towns and cities.** Birds originally hail from the wilderness, so you might imagine that this is the only good place to see them going about their business. One look at the splattered wreckage of auto windshields, public benches, and outdoor hand railings around town will prove otherwise.

4. **Virtually the whole world.** There are very few places on this planet not at least somewhat inhabited by birds. Seriously, they're nearly everywhere. You practically need a submarine to get away from them.

How to Identify Birds

If you are new to birding, species identification can feel difficult and mysterious, but this section is meant to make it more approachable to beginners. If you remember reading this information in one of my previous books, well, read it again. A refresher never hurt anyone.

Of course, people's knowledge levels vary, so if you find yourself thinking, "I already know all of this," then please feel free to jump to the next section with all the other pretentious blowhards.

There are three main areas to consider when attempting to identify a bird:

Bird Parts

An understanding of bird anatomy is key, because much of how we identify species relies on the variations and differences between their parts. Therefore, making yourself familiar with their standard features is recommended.

For the sake of illustration, the sparrow is a good example; as an individual it's very boring, but it has the basic "bird" shape that most people are familiar with. Not all birds look like the sparrow, but trust me, they all have pretty much the same parts.

PARTS of A BIRD

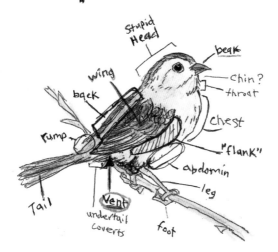

Head: You can probably figure this one out on your own, but it's generally the thing on top of the bird. It's one of the best places to look for the eyes and the beak.

Bill or Beak: No one knows what the difference between a bill and a beak is, but the shape and size is pretty important if you're trying to identify a bird. Pay close attention to this part, because this is what they will peck you blind with if you give them half a chance.

Chin: This may be hard to see on a bird, as most birds are weak-chinned. This suggests they have a weak personality and may lack the willpower to follow projects through to completion.

Throat: Between the chin and the chest. Usually, this is where all that goddamn noise is coming from.

Neck: Most birds don't have enough of a neck to be worth mentioning. Often it's so short that you don't even know it's there. That said, a lot of wading birds have extra long necks. This may give the bird an ungainly appearance, but it's a good place to look for identifying markings. One thing is true of all birds: Short or long, you are never going to see one with a normal-length neck.

Back: Birders should familiarize themselves with the back markings of as many species as possible. Birds have a habit of frequently facing away from you when you're trying to identify them. It's rude.

Chest: Also referred to as the breast. Can be difficult to cook without drying it out.

Abdomen: Goes from the breast down to the undertail. Also called the belly, but not by anyone who's worth taking seriously.

Flanks: This is ornithologist-speak for the sides of a bird. What a bunch of a-holes. Just call it the sides.

Wings: This is the part that makes it a bird. I shouldn't need to explain this.

Rump: The rump is the small area between the back and the tail. Basically, it's the lower back. The rump doesn't really stand out on most birds, though a few species do have unique rump colorations that might be helpful for identification. Go ahead and memorize rump colors for extra credit if you want, but it only makes you a bigger nerd.

Tail: This is the part that sticks off the back of the bird. The variety of shapes, lengths, and colors makes the tail invaluable for identification. Even how the tail is held can tell you a lot about a bird. "Tail up, stuck up" is what I always say.

Vent: It's also called the cloaca, but don't let the fancy terminology fool you; this is the butthole. Birds shit whenever they feel like it, and also whenever they are above your car. The cloaca is also used for laying eggs. Gross.

Undertail Coverts: These are the short feathers under the tail; they may occasionally have colors or markings that could help distinguish between species, but honestly, at this point, who's even looking?

Legs: Length, color, and thickness vary between species, but usually you've already figured it out from literally everything else you can see on the bird. If you want a good laugh some time, try imagining a bird wearing chinos.

Feet: Honestly, I'm not sure a bird has ever been identified by its feet. I only mention them here because they are attached to the bottom of the legs. Bird feet are unattractive.

Foot Fact: Most birds' feet are the same color as their legs, but not all of them! So if you see a bird from a distance and you think it might be wearing shoes, don't say anything, because a lot of ornithologists will never let you live this down.

Bird Size

Another attribute that may help you identify a bird is its size.

Unless you have the proper permits, holding a bird to a ruler is frowned upon. So when judging size, you may find it useful to think of them relative to everyday objects familiar to you. For example, imagine a small, nondescript brown bird. Is it the size of a baseball that you would like to throw over a wall, or more like the size of a golf ball that you would like to hit for about 200 yards? Thrushes and sparrows are roughly baseball-size. If you want to reach for your five iron, it might be a wren.

Bird Shape

Does it have a small body with long, stupid legs, or is it dumpy with a fat head? While no two birds are the same, they all come in one of the six main bird shapes.

THE SIX MAIN
BIRD SHAPES

BASIC

LUMP

ShitSack

FLOATERS

WEIRD LegS

Murder

Section I:

Putting Birds Where They Belong

As many of you already know, I am nothing if not a perfectionist when it comes to categorizing birds.

Geography is one significant and familiar way that species are often organized in field guides, and therefore it will seem logical to many people that I should arrange the birds in this book by region, but those people are wrong.

While I have used geography to organize previous books, science now knows that the birds themselves don't understand maps and frequently refuse to stay at one address. Instead, they flap around from place to place and completely relocate themselves a couple of times a year.

Take the Rose-breasted Grosbeak (*Pheucticus ludovicianus*). If you live in the eastern United States or Canada, they generally show up in the spring and immediately begin to make themselves comfortable around your home. Months pass. Then, just when you've resigned yourself to the company of these colorful members of the cardinal family, they're suddenly off to Mexico, Central America, the Caribbean, and god knows where else. Just like that. They leave without so much as a "goodbye" or a "thanks for letting me disrupt your whole summer with my chattering."

They're like that drifter friend from school who has a lot of travel stories but never seems to have a job, or their own place to stay, and will never pay you back for eating all your sunflower seeds.

Anyway, exactly *where* a bird lives can be very complicated, thanks to their freewheeling nature and lack of common courtesy. Therefore I'm going to keep things simple by grouping the birds according to their primary psychological impact.

Psycho-Impact Groups, or PIGs, are determined using an experimental method that I developed based on certain discoveries made during my inquiries into the arcane ornithological arts; it involves deep meditation in a quiet, dark environment. The meditative state is interrupted at random intervals by flashing images and high-volume audio of each bird, during which I record the first thought or phrase that my subconscious mind supplies in response. The results of multiple sessions are then collated and used to inform the "plain English" group labels used in this book. It is a new field of ornithological study, and very exciting work.

Once the birds have been organized into their respective groups, I then list them in order of how much they suck. This is based on scientifically weighted numerical ratings for each bird.

These numbers are the results of my cutting-edge Bird Universal Mathematical Modeling and Ranking system (BUMMR), which I have spent years fine-tuning and is based on my groundbreaking, though largely unrecognized, Framework for Universal Karmic Ratings (FUKRs).

For the sake of this book, it is not essential for readers to understand the detailed mathematics of this innovative new system, or how exactly it works. But for those who are interested in such things, I have generously included the underlying metrics and the resulting BUMMR score for each bird.

I won't overexplain my methodology here, because that is something that I have been accused of in the past, and I'm not keen to hear the words *abstruse*, *arrogant*, or *borderline* from my editor again if it can be avoided.

Also, my method is proprietary, so, actually, don't even ask me.

I do recognize that this organizational system is a bit of a departure from most bird guides. So, for that reason, at the end of this book I have also included the traditional geographic bird regions and provided a corresponding index of the birds, for those who need to be reassured that the world is still under control and that everything is going to be okay.

If you believe there is a better system, or would like to recommend another approach for my future books, please feel free to send me your typewritten rant via post to the following address:

> Literary Suggestions Department
> C/O Municipal Recycling & Shredding Ctr.
> 7768677 Noh Way
> New York, NM 510468927

Section 2:

The Birds

This is the section with all the birds in it.

Each entry in this section features a description of a bird, its behaviors, and other relevant information. The text is paired with an illustration for visual reference.

The birds have been grouped into broad categories defined by their primary effect on the human psyche. And, for the first time ever, species are now measured using my new, highly innovative BUMMR analysis. It's not an exact science (yet), but I believe it will provide the reader with valuable insight into the personality of each bird.

"Yes," you say, "but why *these* birds and not some other birds? Aren't all birds worthy of your study in the exciting-yet-nascent field of Scientific Bird Critique?"

Simply put, yes. But I believe that *these* birds deserve it more than the others, and it's high time they received the spotlight. The other birds out there can wait, at least until these particular miscreants are exposed for who they really are.

A Flock of A–holes

Bleak–bill Magpie

Pica hudsonia

Common Name: Black–billed Magpie, American Magpie

A lot of Americans probably once felt that, regardless of our shortcomings, at least we didn't have magpies in our country. Not like those unfortunate Brits.

But, in 1804, explorers Lewis and Clark noticed that there were magpies in South Dakota. They turned out to be American Magpies and, just like that, our brief period of cultural superiority vanished in a puff of New World smoke.

We now call *Pica hudsonia* the Black-billed Magpie rather than the American Magpie. It deflects some of the shame of having them at all, but ultimately there is no denying that they are endemic to most of the Midwest and western United States.

Their range extends north to Alaska, spilling over a vast swath of Canada along the way like grape juice spilled on your carpet by a neighbor's out-of-control child as they run through the living room at a birthday party. (Sorry, Canada—kids, am I right?)

Like many Americans, the Black-billed Magpie is an opportunistic omnivore who will eat as much as possible of just about anything they can. Seeds, berries, rodents, carrion, unattended pet food, you name it . . . even garbage.

Of course, they're not just indiscriminate about their food; they are also dicks—Black-billed Magpies are shameless nest

bleak-bill
Magpie

Range MAP
(pica hudsonia)

MAGPIES →

Lewis & Clark

S. America
(magpie free

"Discovered" magpies in South Dakota.

(Nice work, dillholes.)

predators who steal eggs from other birds' nests like they are entitled to them.

As if their lack of empathy for others wasn't enough, these birds are also terrible to each other—within flocks, dominant magpies often steal food from social subordinates, just because they can.

Americans, am I right?

Description: *Black with striking white underbellies, shoulders, and primary wing tips, which can be seen only in flight. A bit flashy for what is basically a crow, if you ask me.*

Bird Region: Midwestern United States and most of western North America, I'm afraid

BUMMR RATING

Aggression:	+4.0
Entitlement:	+5.0
Bad manners:	+20.0
Canada:	−8.0
Typical Americanness:	21.0

Blow Jay

Cyanocitta cristata
Common Name: Blue Jay

This big, noisy bastard is well known to anyone who lives in eastern North America, and can be seen from southern Canada to the tip of Florida.

They migrate in flocks by the thousands, but scientists are uncertain exactly how individual birds decide whether to migrate each season. We'll probably never know because jays are an unruly bunch of jackwads whose only organizing principle seems to be "fuck you."

Blue Jays are easily identified by their loud, abrasive calls and their characteristic blue, white, and black markings. That, and those obnoxious, perky blue crests, which they're always raising expressively at you because they think it's charming.

Like all jays, they are mouthy assholes with inflated egos.

Backyard Tip: *These guys looove acorns, so if you value your peace and quiet, don't move into a home anywhere near an oak tree.*

Bird Region: Pretty much the whole right half of North America

Blow Jay

BUMMR RATING

Planning ahead:	-3.0
Friendliness:	-17.0
Always yelling:	-29.0

Bird Assessment: *Asshole*

BIRD ASSESSMENT · ASSHOLE · BIRD ASSESSMENT

Bum Snaggle

Hirundo rustica
Common Name: Barn Swallow, Swallow

The Barn Swallow is probably the most common swallow in the whole world. They can be found swooping and wheeling dangerously close to the ground in their pursuit of flying insects across open spaces just about everywhere.

In fact, if you have ever visited an open field in North America, Europe, Asia, South America, Africa, Southeast Asia, or even northern Australia, then you have probably seen these swoopy little bug-eating jagoffs trying to catch a mouthful of flies as they careen through the air like wild teenagers behind the wheel of a sports car. It's pure reckless endangerment.

American ornithologist Arthur Cleveland Bent wrote in his seminal series *Life Histories of Familiar North American Birds*, "Everybody who notices birds at all knows, admires, and loves the graceful, friendly barn swallow."

What a fat load of crap. No responsible adult could admire this stupid, bug-sucking menace of a bird. It's only a matter of time before someone is killed.

Anyway, you can sort of forgive Bent because later, in the same twenty-page entry on Barn Swallows, he fondly reminisces, "I once had a large, black cat that was a great bird catcher . . . one day I saw him leap into the air and catch a swallow, as it swooped low over the grass tops."

At least he had good taste in cats.

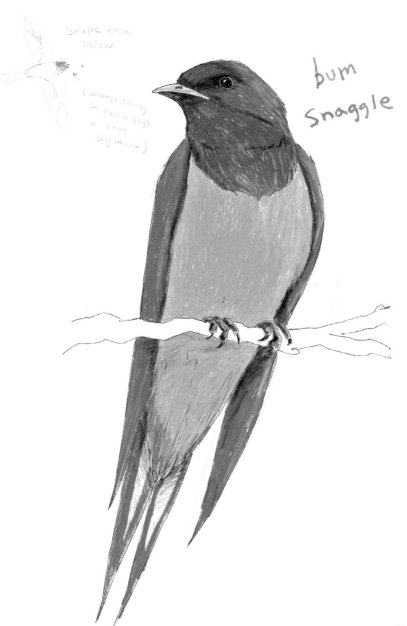

snipe from
below

(always trying
to catch bugs
in that
big mouth)

bum
snaggle

39

- Housecats can jump 6-8 feet
- Swallows swoop around ~0-75 feet

75'

0'

Cat Zone of opportunity

PSS PSS PSS

good names for cats

1. Michael Jordan
2. Mr. Jumpers
3. Dr. John Swatson
4. ~~Jeff Pounders~~
5. Sir Leaps-a-Lot
6. Juan Pounce de Le
7. Christopher Stalker
8. Sir Claw-rence Olivier

Identification: *Barn Swallows are identifiable by their deep-blue upperparts, rufous face, and that stupid, distinctive forked "swallow tail" that they are so proud of for some reason.*

Bird Region: Oh my god, like everywhere

```
BUMMR RATING

SWALLOW QUALITIES
  Is it too reckless?                       YES
  from 0-10:                                 -9
  Is it too swoopy?                         YES
  from 0-10:                                 -9
  Can't seem to get away from them:         -20

REDEEMING QUALITIES
  Inspires high achievement in cats:         +1
```

Judgement:	*Guilty.*

Comments: Consistently exhibits poor decision-making, willful disregard for safety of others, and shows no remorse for actions.

Recommended sentence: 18 months' detention, juvenile hall.

Chestnut Wing Kook-a-loo

Clamator coromandus

Common Name: Chestnut-winged Cuckoo

Get a load of this screwball.

The Chestnut-winged Cuckoo is, surprise, a cuckoo with chestnut-colored wings. Man, the Department of Bird Naming was really phoning it in that day, weren't they?

These cuckoos are long tailed and have slate-colored backs with a thin white collar below their black head and that wild, unbelievably disheveled crest.

Throw in that stupid downturned beak and this bird suddenly looks like an aging Rod Stewart impersonator who is depressed about his growing inability to book a decent gig.

Like many other cuckoos, the Chestnut-winged Cuckoo practices brood parasitism—this means, when they breed, the female secretly lays her eggs in the nest of another bird because she doesn't want the trouble and expense of raising her own young. These cuckoos lay their eggs primarily in the unattended nests of various species of laughing thrushes and then fly away thinking, "Who's laughing now, thrushes?"

If this seems like a dick move, that's because it is.

Bird Region: India, Asia, Indonesia (in the Himalayas and scattered across much of Asia, as far west as Japan)

Chestnut Wing Kookaloo

BUMMR RATING

Dependable parent:	*-37*
Hairstyle:	*-13*
Singing career:	*Rock bottom.*

Chances of redemption: *None*

Hoodlum Merganser

Lophodytes cucullatus
Common Name: Hooded Merganser

This duck is small and looks like trouble.

In fact, this tiny motherfucker just looks straight-up crazy. Seriously, look at those eyes. Those eyes say, "I might seem cute now, but I will fuck you up if you look at me wrong."

If ever there was a bird who might be concealing a switchblade or a chain under its leather jacket, the Hooded Merganser would be it. Never trust a duck with a pompadour.

Bird Region: Common in small rivers and ponds across most of North America

hoodlum
Merganser

BUMMR RATING

Appears cute:	*+18*
Crazy eyes:	*-13*
Potential for violence:	*??*
Suspicious hairstyle:	*-2*

Trustability total: Watch your back

Stuperb Starling

Lamprotornis superbus
Common Name: Superb Starling

There are exceptions to the fashion rule that blue and brown make a bad color combination, and the so-called Superb Starling is not one of them.

They do have a striking black cap and mask, but unfortunately (and rather embarrassingly) this small passerine appears to have been mismeasured for its plumage, because I see Paris, I see France, I see the clearly defined white gap between its blue breast and brown underparts. If I'm honest, this color-challenged dud looks like he's wearing ill-fitted suit separates and has his briefs on display for god and everyone to see. In terms of fashion, this is actually the opposite of superb.

Common to woodlands, scrublands, savanna, and villages across most of East Africa, they can be found in small flocks, usually making a variety of noisy scolds and shrieks at anyone within earshot.

I guess that's just the nature of their personalities, but if my shirt didn't reach my pants, I would try to avoid drawing unnecessary attention to myself.

Bird Region: East Africa

Stuperb Starling

BUMMR RATING

Fashion (blue + brown):	-3
I see Paris, I see France:	-8
Scolding/shrieking:	-45
Superb?	*No*

BIRD ASSESSMENT
DUMBFUCK
BIRD ASSESSMENT

Conceited Bastards

Blank Staring-eyes Flycrapper

Terpsiphone atrocaudata

Common Name: Black Paradise Flycatcher, Japanese Paradise Flycatcher

With his glossy black-crested head, dark purplish wings, and long, black tail feathers, the Black Paradise Flycatcher's plumage could be called attention grabbing—but it is the vivid, neon blue eye rings that really stand out.

He looks like he's trying to put you into a hypnotic trance with the intensity of his gaze . . . but the harder he stares, the more he comes off like a cut-rate magician in a gaudy tailcoat suffering from stage fright. He's pathetic. If he had a mustache, it would no doubt be coming unglued right now.

Also called the Japanese Paradise Flycatcher, these medium-size passerines breed mainly in the forests of Japan and South Korea, but their range spreads west and as far south as Malaysia during migration.

There is not much else to say about this bird, other than he's not hypnotizing anyone.

Bird Region: Currently attempting to mesmerize southeastern Asia

Blank staring-eyes
flyCrapper

tail length = too long?

BUMMR RATING

Dressed for the part: -3
Stage presence: -8
_____

Hypnotic ability: *Give it up*

Desplendent qu'est-ce que c'est?

Pharomachrus mocinno
Common Name: Resplendent Quetzal

The Resplendent Quetzal is truly remarkable for the staggering amount of garish flamboyance packed into such a small amount of bird. Only the male is crested, but both sexes wear an overcomplicated plumage of iridescent greens, jewel-red bellies, and glossy black wings.

They specialize in eating wild avocados, and are shy, cautious birds who stay quiet much of the time in order to avoid unwanted attention from predators.

However, showboating in that "jewel-like" plumage seems counterproductive to hiding, so it's not surprising that they're everybody's favorite meal, being preyed on by owls, hawks, and eagles, as well as toucanets, jays, weasels, squirrels, and even a member of the raccoon family (an adorable rascal known as the honey bear, who apparently relishes eating quetzal eggs).

You would almost feel some sympathy for these glittering losers, if people weren't constantly gushing about how beautiful they are. Resplendent, my ass.

Bird Region: From the southernmost tip of Mexico all the way to western Panama

don't choke
on that avocado,
stupid

Desplendent
qu'est-ce que c'est?

BIRD
ASSESSMENT
LOSER

BUMMR RATING

Fucking show-off:	-80
Good eating, apparently:	+10
Redeeming qualities?:	-70

Lame-bow Bee-eater

Merops ornatus

Common Name: Rainbow Bee-eater

This unnecessarily colorful little prick lives on a diet of flying insects. Oh, and in case it wasn't obvious from their painfully unimaginative name, they have a thing for eating bees, which sucks, because bees are amazing.

The Rainbow Bee-eater can be found all over southern Australia in the summer. In the winter they migrate to northern Australia, though sometimes they travel as far north as Indonesia.

Like all bee-eaters, they are ground nesters who dig burrows to lay their eggs in. One interesting thing about this is that if you can fly, why the hell don't you build your stupid nest up in a tree where someone isn't going to accidentally trip on it while they're out for a walk?

Rainbow Bee-eaters only breed before or after Australia's rainy season, presumably because, if it rained, they would drown in their own stupid nest holes.

Fun Fact: *Ground-nesting birds are stupid.*

Bird Region: Australia, mate

lame-bow
bee eater

BUMMR RATING

Nests in holes/is stupid:	-10
Easy food for cats:	+10
Attention seeking (colors):	-10
Stays in Australia:	+10
Eats bees:	-100

Bird assessment:	-100
	(fail)

Northern Dorkingbird

Mimus polyglottos

Common Name: Northern Mockingbird

This small passerine bird was once a popular pet to keep. God knows why, because they are boring to look at and they won't stop singing.

But they were so popular that the trade in caged mockingbirds threatened their existence. Then, with the passage of the Migratory Bird Treaty Act of 1918, that threat slowly petered out and *Mimus polyglottos* made a comeback—so much so that today it can be found singing its dumb lungs out across most of the United States. I guess you can't win 'em all.

Like other mockingbirds, this one is an insufferable show-off, constantly mimicking other species just because it can. In fact, if you have ever been disturbed by what sounded like a series of ten or fifteen various birds taking turns yammering outside your window, there's a very good chance that you were just being harassed by a Northern Mockingbird.

Description: *Their singing is considered colorful, but really, these birds are just drab gray assholes.*

Bird Region: North America, and I mean a lot of it. It is a year-round resident from the midwestern United States to the south through Mexico.

BUMMR RATING

Visual interest:	+0
Mocking:	+42
Showing off:	+12

Hateworthiness:	54
	(Fuck off,
	already)

Northern
dorkingbird

Ooh-lah-lah Cockydoo

Eolophus roseicapilla
Common Name: Galah, Galah Cockatoo, Pink and Grey
Cockatoo, Rose-breasted Cockatoo

Common to nearly all parts of Australia, this big pink-and-gray show-off is the reigning champion of Bad Hairstyles for Parrots. (Another common Australian parrot, Major Mitchell's Cockatoo, was also in the running, but in the end, it took first prize for Birds Who Look Like Members of a Village People Tribute Band instead.)

Galah feed on the ground, eating seeds and grasses, and they thrive in a wide variety of habitats throughout the Australian continent. These raucous little puff-heads can be found in groups ranging from just a few birds to massive flocks, and are known for being "energetic," which usually is just another way of saying "noisy." In urban areas they are common in parks and gardens, and they seem to even enjoy the company of humans.

I have never been to Australia, but this sounds like a god-damn nightmare.

Bird Region: Australia, and it's bloody full of the pink bastards

BUMMR RATING

Hairstyle:	12.5
Personality:	7.2
Pink + gray:	8.0
Noise:	11.0
Energy/attitude:	9.1
Local ubiquity:	8.6
Cockatoo index:	56.4

Recommendation: mild
sedatives when visiting
Australia

oh-la-lah
Cocky-doo

Sultan Twit

Melanochlora sultanea
Common Name: Sultan Tit

This tit needs to get the fuck over himself. *Melanochlora sultanea* is a small and unreasonably showy black-and-yellow narcissist, native to the Indomalayan realm.[*]

There are four recognized subspecies of *M. sultanea*, and they are all completely in love with the sound of their own voices. Vocalizations are varied, and include a squeaky and annoyingly repetitive "chwek-chwek," a vapid "CHEEK-Piu-Piu-Piu-Piu" call, and sometimes an intense, piercingly high-pitched scream of, just, like, "CHEEEEEEEE!!"

That last one goes right through your nerves like an ice pick.

The Sultan Tit forages for caterpillars and berries high in the forest canopy, and, oh my god, I hate him.

Description: *A dark face, throat, and upperparts are contrasted by striking yellow underparts and that stupid, cocky yellow crest that he raises in alarm whenever he thinks he's not getting enough attention.*

Bird Region: Indomalaya—don't worry about it

---

[*] Indomalaya stretches across the Indian subcontinent, most of South and Southeast Asia, and the southern parts of East Asia. It is a "biogeographic realm," which has to do with distributional patterns of organisms, and don't worry, I'm not going to explain it to you. All you really need to know is that some scientists decided to divide up the world into a bunch of realms, so now we have Indomalaya.

Sultan twit

BUMMR RATING

Stupidness of calls:	+10
Piercing-ness of calls:	+10
Repetitiveness of calls:	+10 +10 +10
Thinks he's so attractive:	+150

How much I hate this bird: *You have no idea.*

Headaches with Feathers

Common Night-honk

Chordeiles minor

Common Name: Common Nighthawk, Bulbat

Found throughout the Americas, Common Nighthawks are actually members of the nightjar family, which are sometimes called goatsuckers (big shudder).

They are crepuscular, meaning they just sit around on a branch all day. They only become active during the twilight hours, just before sunrise, and then again just after sunset. That's like, what, two or three hours a day? Lazy-ass birds.

When they finally do get off their branches, they fly around acting like bats, flapping and looping and trying to catch insects in flight. They have laughably small beaks, but huge, freakish, yawning mouths that open really, really wide. This may be useful when you're trying to suck down a lot of bugs, but it's rude to fly with your mouth open. Plus, seeing a big, gaping bird maw coming your way will give anyone a case of the creeps.

If all that isn't unsettling enough for you, these bastards are also known for "booming." Booming is a display behavior where the male hurtles himself toward the ground in a high-speed dive, which he only pulls out of about three feet short of ending up a smoking, feathery wreck.

"So what?" you say. "Lots of birds are reckless and stupid."

Yes, but here's the thing: During their dive, just as the air traveling though their wing tips creates an alarming sound of its own, the Nighthawk delivers a loud, high-pitched nasal

Common
night-honk

bugs

Lazy

. "crepuscular"

. reckless

65

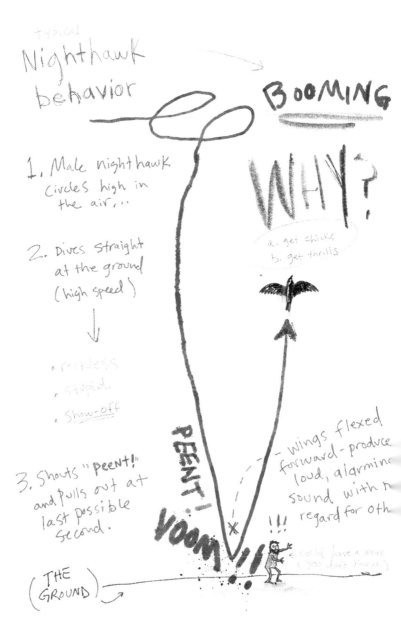

typical
Nighthawk behavior

BOOMING

1. Male nighthawk circles high in the air...

2. Dives straight at the ground (high speed)

↓

• reckless
• stupid
• show-off

3. Shouts "PEENT!" and pulls out at last possible second.

PEENT!

VOOM!!!

THE GROUND →

WHY?
a. get chicks
b. get thrills

- wings flexed forward - produce loud, alarming sound with no regard for oth

!!!

could have a heart attack (you don't know)

call. Imagine the sound of a Formula 1 race car if it shrieked past you from behind in the dark.

"PEEENT!!" VOOOOOOMMM!

You try taking an evening walk past a field where a bunch of nighthawks are booming. It's fucking unnerving. I hope you took your heart medicine.

Bird Region: All over the Americas

BUMMR RATING

Slothfulness (day):	*-23.0*
Recklessness (night):	*-12.3*
Disregard for others:	*-13.5*
Enjoyability:	*-48.8*

Crusty Tit

Lophophanes cristatus

Common Name: Crested Tit, European Crested Tit

These tiny tits belong to the passerine family Paridae, which includes tits, chickadees, and titmice, so go ahead, get out all of your adolescent snickering and then try to behave like an adult, if it's not too much to ask.

The European Crested Tit (settle down . . .) can be found throughout Northern and Central Europe, as well as parts of Southern Europe. In the United Kingdom they live almost exclusively in Scotland.

They thrive in deep forest, but they are lousy at traversing unwooded terrain, so populations tend to remain in the same small area and rarely expand beyond it. This explains why there are a lot of these tits in the highland pine forests of Scotland and almost none in the rest of Great Britain (putting to bed any notion that the Scots are just hoarding these irritating little shits for some reason).

This bird is very small but incredibly annoying. Its call could be described as bubbly, high pitched, and way too fucking chattery.

Description: *Buff/brown body with a pale head ringed in black and a distinctive crest that we are supposed to be impressed by. Like all birds with crests, these tits love to show them off to anyone who will look.*

Bird Region: Europe, obviously

crusty
tit

BUMMR RATING

Volume level "low":	*+1*
Very high pitched:	*-45*
Won't shut up:	*-75*
Personality *"bubbly"*:	*-100*
Weight (approximate):	*0.4 oz.*
	(11 g)

Irritation-to-weight ratio: *547.5*
("extreme")

Eurasian Butthunch

Sitta europaea

Common Name: Eurasian Nuthatch, Wood Nuthatch, Nuthatch

Nuthatches. These energetic passerines are a bit like wood-peckers, if woodpeckers were tiny and neurotic.

Like woodpeckers, nuthatches can cling to and negotiate tree trunks vertically. But while the woodpeckers are hugging bark and drilling for grubs, these hyperactive twits never stop moving, perpetually running around like sugar-mad children at a birthday party.

Up! Down! Upside down! Downside up! Which way am I going? Ha ha! I don't know! Faster!

Like all nuthatches, they nest in cavities, but the Eurasian Nuthatch is known for choosing abandoned woodpecker holes. Make your own nest? Nah. They've gotta get back to skittering around trees like maniacs and shouting at each other with their loud, insistent calls. It's like they're jacked up on candy and prescription stimulants.

Identification: *Small, compact bodies with buff or white underparts. Slate-blue back, wings, and tail, and a distinctive black eye mask. Actually, they look suspiciously similar to some North American nuthatches I know. It figures. Those guys are nuts, too.*

Bird Region: Most of temperate Europe and Asia

BUMMR RATING

Attention to detail:	*-10*
Which way am I going?:	*-10*
Listening to others?:	*-10*
Hahahahahaha:	*-10*
Neurotic Chaos:	*100%*

Eurasian butthunch

Dowdy Woodfucker

Dryobates pubescens

Common Name: Downy Woodpecker

This might be the smallest woodpecker in North America. Who knows? It's like a smaller version of a real woodpecker. You might be one of those people who think miniature versions of animals are cute, but in this case you'd be wrong. Because, trust me, it's not so cute when this little bastard starts hammering away at the tree outside your bedroom window before your alarm clock even goes off.

It is a year-round resident in most of Canada and the United States. Unlike most woodpeckers, you might find this pint-size dick in your backyard, mixing with the chickadees and eating seeds or suet from your feeder. He's too lazy to dig bugs out of trees like a regular woodpecker if he can sponge food off of someone else instead.

Description: *Smaller than a robin, but just as dumb. Looks like a woodpecker.*

Bird Region: Seems like everywhere (North America)

dowdy woodfucker

```
BUMMR RATING

Small for a woodpecker:         +5
Still a woodpecker:            -50
Mooching off chickadees:       x1.1
───────────────────────────────────
Achievement Score:           -49.5
                           (failing)
───────────────────────────────────
```

Notes: Underperforms at basic woodpeckering.

What the Hell-bird

Procnias albus

Common Name: White Bellbird

With its pure white body and striking black beak, the White Bellbird could be described as attractive, except for the long, weird-looking wattle coming right out of the middle of its fucking face.

It just hangs there, dangling in the wind like a gross, limp, sparsely feathered worm. I guess it's meant to attract mates, but if you ask me, it just says, "STAY AWAY!"

I admit the wattle does command attention, though. I mean, you can't take your eyes off the thing. It's hypnotic and nauseating all at the same time.

In spite of the monstrosity growing out of its forehead, the thing that makes this bird truly abominable is its excruciating mating call, a piercing metallic ringing sound. Seriously, it's like Thor's hammer hitting an anvil, only WAY too loud.

"Oh, come now," you say. "We all know that loud bird calls are annoying. How bad can this one really be?"

Well, let me put it in perspective for you:

•   Normal human conversation is about 65 decibels.

•   Gas-powered leaf blowers are 80 to 85 decibels; this can damage your hearing after about two hours of exposure.

db = "decibels" — decibel is the unit of
measure for the loudness
or intensity of sound.

* It is LOGARITHMIC, meaning that a 10 d
increase represents a doubling in
how LOUD it sounds.

blah
blah
blah

= 65 db

normal conversation
(mostly boring, but
reasonable volumes.)

Alarm clock
80 db

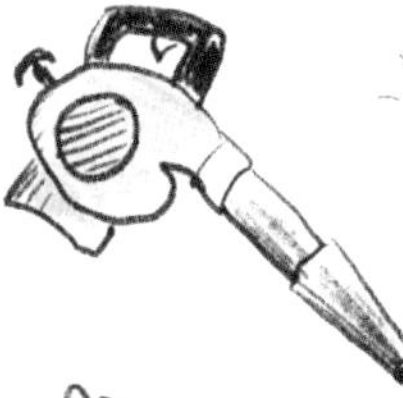

= 85 db

using a
gas powered
leaf blower

ROCK ON!

= 120 db

ROCK CONCERTS
without hearing
protection
(stupid)

= fuck off

* 125 decibels is 22
(twenty...two!) time
louder than an
ALARM CLOCK.

- Your average rock concert is a whopping 90 to 120 decibels, which is why everyone in Metallica wears earplugs but still responds to questions from the press with "WHAT?"

- Meanwhile, this ear-piercing tropical prick, the bellbird, is the loudest bird ever recorded by scientists, blasting out its hellish calls at an *ear-busting 125 decibels*. That, by the way, just happens to be the volume level that causes physical pain and results in instant hearing loss for humans. Coincidence? I doubt it.

Fun Fact: This bird is a dangerous nuisance and should be jailed for noise ordinance violations.

Bird Region: Parts of Venezuela, Guyana, Suriname, French Guiana, Brazil, and the islands of Trinidad and Tobago. Can be heard from just about anywhere, though, I imagine.

```
BUMMR RATING

Slick plumage:                              +5
Nausea worm:                               -20
Possible hearing loss:                    -125
```

```
Enjoyability equivalent:        Permanent tinnitus
```

Wastes of Feathers

Blah-strich

Struthio camelus

Common Name: Common Ostrich

This awkward-looking son of a bitch is the largest and heaviest living bird on this planet. While average height and weight varies by population, males can stand up to 9 feet (2.74 meters) tall and weigh over 300 pounds (136 kilograms). Standard weights and measures aside, that is a fuck-ton of ugly bird.

In addition to being way too tall, the Common Ostrich is a walking tribute to bad design. Giant, gangly legs, fat brown body, tiny wings, long, skinny neck . . . and, to top it all off, a laughably small head. If you detect a look of stupidity in its billiard ball–size eyes, it's probably because each one is larger than its brain.

Fun Fact: *Ostriches can't fly, but they are incredibly fast on land, easily sustaining speeds of over 30 miles per hour while they hold their sad little wings out to the sides and run. Some experts believe this behavior may help them with balance when making turns, but I think it's probably just the closest sensation to flying that these giant dimwits will ever get.*

Bird Region: Native to Africa, wild ostriches can also be found in Australia, where some escaped captivity and have become feral. Yes, you heard that right: feral ostriches. Goddammit, Australia.

BUMMR RATING

Tallness:	-7.2
Stupidness:	-9.7
Flavor:	-0.3
	(gamey)
Loveable?:	-17.2
	(FAIL)

blah-
strich

you get
the idea

Brown-crap Rosy-finch

Leucosticte australis
Common Name: Brown-capped Rosy Finch

This bird has the smallest breeding territory of all the rosy finches—its migratory range is basically limited to a high-altitude mountainous area of Colorado. That's the good news.

Otherwise, *Leucosticte australis* is just a medium-size finch that spends its whole life doing tediously boring finch stuff, like eating seeds and whatever. Seriously, it's too boring to even think about.

The Brown-capped Rosy Finch makes its nest in the rocky crannies of sheer cliff faces. While it is capable of building a nest in as little as three days, it often takes much longer—sometimes upward of two weeks! Why? Maybe because the nesting material keeps getting fucking blown off the rocks by the constant gusts of high mountain winds, and they have to keep starting over from scratch.

A little advice: Next time, try building your home in a less windy crevice, dipshit.

***Color:** Brown and pink, nature's worst color combo*

Bird Region: High up in the Rocky Mountains. Let's hope they stay there.

BUMMR RATING

Stays in the mountains:	*+10*
Color combo:	*-3*
Real estate instincts:	*-7*
Interestingness:	*+0*
Reasons to exist:	*0*

BIRD
ASSESSMENT
DUMBFUCK
BIRD
ASSESSMENT

brown-crap
rosy-finch

Cruddy Turdstone

Arenaria interpres

Common Name: Ruddy Turnstone

A short, turd-shaped wading bird who breeds in the northern tundras of Eurasia and North America, the Turnstone hangs around up and down coastlines everywhere during the nonbreeding season.

The Ruddy Turnstone is considered cosmopolitan—not cosmopolitan like they're all sporting the latest fashion while they sip martinis and discuss French New Wave film in swanky bars. Ha ha, no, these birds are not stylish or fun.

A cosmopolitan species is one that can be found worldwide, residing just about anywhere there is a suitable habitat. In other words, they are not very discerning.

Arenaria interpres has a slightly upturned bill, which might convey a certain grace, if this bird didn't spend most of its time with that upturned bill shoved into the sand, flipping up stones and wads of seaweed in an undignified bid to find a small insect or crustacean to eat. Given the chance, it's also not above sticking that sandy beak into the odd gull egg. What a dick.

Fun Fact: *Turnstones used to be considered part of the Plover family, but the genus,* Arenaria, *is now placed in the Sandpiper family, which means, who cares?*

Bird Region: Coastlines everywhere in the world are blighted with this bird.

BUMMR RATING

Style:	+0
Panache:	+0
Importance:	+0
Cleanliness:	-3

This bird is cruddy.

Cruddy
Turdstone

Green Pissant

Phasianus versicolor

Common Name: Green Pheasant, Japanese Green Pheasant, Kiji

With patterned pale gray wings and long tail, a striking bottle-green body, jewellike blue-green head, and bright red face wattles, this pheasant is a real pain in the eyes. It's the national bird of Japan, where they are widespread and known as "kiji."

The kiji is significant in Japanese history and culture, and it appears in a popular folktale about a boy named Momotarō, who was apparently born from a peach and grew up to fight demons with a magic mallet. Damn, that's pretty cool.

Momotarō has a band of animals who help him on his journey, including a dog, a monkey, and a *green pheasant*. Interesting choice, because do you know what pheasants do when there is danger? They "flush," which is just pheasant slang for "get flustered and fly away at top speed."

Someone please tell me how *that* is supposed to be helpful in a mallet brawl with demons. Honestly, it seems like one good dog and a marginally effective monkey would be more than adequate. I don't really get what a jittery bird brings to the team.

Some say kiji are extremely sensitive to tremors and once provided people with valuable early warnings in an earthquake-prone region. Of course that's of no use in demon combat, so we can safely say that the value of this bird's "special sensitivity" has been near zero since the invention of seismographs in the 1870s.

national bird of Japan!
+ maybe detects tremors?
– useless in a fight.

green pissant

If you ever get to choose your own demon-fighting team:

DOG!
- Loyal
- Good natured
- Sense of smell
- Can bite
- good dog!

SOLID CHOICE

✓ yes!

An Oni is a kind of demon sometimes called an ogre or troll in Japanese folklore

1. They are BAD LUCK and TROUBLE

Monkey
- Smart
- agile
- irrepressible scamp!
- mischievous
- can bite, steal stuff,
- swing from trees

EXCELLENT!

✓ hell yeah!

2. They are known for their super-human strength and big-ass clubs.

pheasant   ✗
- senses earthquakes?
- flushes at first hint of danger

what? no.

choose your hunters wisely.

In spite of its pretentious plumage, fragile nerves, and apparent uselessness in a fight, the green pheasant *is* still Japan's national bird and a beloved character in Japanese folk history.

Also, it's one of only twenty-nine animals that can be legally hunted in Japan, which is confusing because it's usually frowned upon, if not outright illegal, to shoot your own national bird. Japan is a complicated place.

Bird Region: Japan

```
BUMMR RATING

Dog friend:                                      +100
Monkey friend:                                   +100
Is bird:                                         -150
Value to team in fight:                          ????
Predicts earthquakes:                           Maybe
_____
Subtotal:                                     Unknown
_____
MOMOTARŌ DEMON TEAM:                            x1000
_____
Confusion rating:       >[ERROR: CANNOT CALCULATE]
```

Lark Buttnick

Calamospiza melanocorys

Common Name: Lark Bunting

Foraging on the ground for grains, seeds, and insects, this little North American sparrow typically avoids feeding under cover, which seems remarkably stupid, because the Lark Bunting would make an ideal snack for busy hawks and eagles on the go.

They have a sizable range that starts in Mexico, traverses the North American continent, and, during breeding, gets jammed right up into Canada like an unexpected dog nose in the crotch. They stick mostly to meadows, prairies, and desert environments throughout the year, breeding in the dry shrubsteppe of the Great Plains.

Wait, hold on. We have a *shrubsteppe*?!

Yes! But unfortunately, *shrubsteppe* is not the German word for the endless, windswept barrens between earth and the afterlife, where failed poets are banished to be eternally lonely after they die. It's actually just a certain kind of flat, treeless, low-rainfall grassland ecosystem, which is more like an endless, windswept nowheresville. Either way, I guess it seems like a reasonable place to find the Lark Bunting.

Breeding males have a bluish-gray bill. They are black bodied and have a stark white patch on their wings, but it's not that great. Put it this way: It's going to take a lot more than some half-assed, colorless wing markings to get anyone jazzed about another low-IQ sparrow.

lark
buttnick

NOTE:
found in
Shrubsteppe!
just grass.

Draw a Lark bunting
the Dumb Birds way

Shrubsteppe

Lark buntings

Low I.Q. birds

Start with this easy to remember Venn diagram.

two circles

SO EASY! anyone can do it

why would they want

Who knows maybe they bored.

draw the thing

add wings + head and stuff

DONE! POINTLESS!

1   2   3

Bird-watching Tip: *If you're trying to spot one of these small birds, scan the shrubsteppe for small areas that are black and white and pointless. That's a Lark Bunting.*

Bird Region: Right up the old shrubsteppe

BUMMR RATING

Black-and-white markings:	*Eh.*
It's a sparrow:	*Boring.*
Shrubsteppe just dry grass:	*VERY disappointing.*

Overall rating: ★☆☆☆☆
Would not recommend.

Magnolia Bungler

Setophaga magnolia

Common Name: Magnolia Warbler

Setophaga magnolia breeds in the dense conifer forests of Canada but can be seen in the eastern half of the United States during the migratory season, when they make their way down to winter in southern Mexico, Central America, and the Caribbean.

Though tiny, this boreal warbler is not difficult to spot—the male's striking, high-contrast yellow-and-black markings would make this dumbfuck conspicuous even if he weren't constantly warbling his lungs out. WEETA-WEETA-WHEEEE-EEEEEAT! It's goddamn never-ending.

Males and females work together to build a nest of thin grasses and twigs. Nests are usually placed on a horizontal conifer branch less than 10 feet above the ground, which makes sense, given the careless, rickety appearance of their design. No one would be surprised if the occasional fledgling fell through a poorly constructed wall.

> **Bird Fact:** *The scientific name, Setophaga, comes from the ancient Greek words for "moth" and "eating," but the Magnolia Warbler is not so choosey; in addition to moths, caterpillars, butterflies, fruit, and spiders, this idiot is also known for eating parts of fir branches.*

Bird Region: North and Central America, plus the Caribbean

Magnolia Bungler

```
BUMMR RATING

Brains:                             n/a
Looks:              Too much yellow?
Construction skills:                0.3
All that warbling:                -14.0
────────────────────────────────────────
Bird-watchability:                -13.7
            (Sigh, "No thank you.")
```

Weak-bellied Geek Pudgeon

Treron sieboldii

Common Name: White-bellied Green Pigeon

With its bright green upper body, olive wings, and white underparts, this medium-size member of the Columbidae family is a real eye-catcher, but not in a good way.

Their light bluish beak, if we're being honest, clashes with their bright green breast, and the white plumage on their underparts and legs gives the general impression of "I'm not wearing pants!" which is something nobody wants to see.

Pigeons in general are not the brightest birds on the perch, but the White-bellied Green Pigeon seems intent on proving it, because *these fashion-challenged fuckwits drink seawater*. Scientists believe this might somehow help with their digestion of certain acidic berries, but I think the more plausible explanation is that these birds are just monumentally dim.

Note: *No one asked for another pigeon.*

Bird Region: They can be found guzzling salt water and strutting around like half-dressed idiots in Japan, China, and many parts of East and Southeast Asia.

Weak-bellied geek pudgeon

BUMMR RATING

Fashion sense:	−5
Colorful for a pigeon:	+10
Is still a pigeon:	−5
Need for another pigeon:	0.0

Should-flush

Hylocichla mustelina
Common Name: Wood Thrush

Like most thrushes, the Wood Thrush is boring.

Look at this boring-ass brown bird. It is mostly brown on top and has a fat-looking white belly covered in boring brown spots.

The male and female look very similar to one another, making it hard to distinguish between them. But that doesn't matter because no one can keep their attention trained on one of these boring shits for more than a second or two, anyway.

Some say that the male's song is the most beautiful of all the thrushes. What does that even mean?

Description: *I've already forgotten what it looks like.*

Bird Region: Generally the right half of North America, but during the winter, *H. mustelina* heads south to bore the hell out of Mexico and Central America.

Should-flush

BUMMR RATING

Boringness:	+900
Brown:	+10
Bore score:	910
	("100% Condensed Boredom")

Creeps and Weirdos

Blech-neck Dweeb

Podiceps nigricollis

Common Name: Black-necked Grebe, Eared Grebe

Oh. My. God. This bird *eats its own feathers*.

Actually, it turns out that all grebes eat their own feathers. I know, right? Why would anyone do that?

The prevailing theory is that the ingested feathers help slow the passage of food on its way through the grebe, allowing their diet of aquatic insects and tiny crustaceans more time to liquify in the stomach. Indigestible material is trapped in the feathers and then regurgitated, thus protecting the grebe's delicate digestive track.

Here's another theory: Fucking gross! What a freak. I mean, get a load of this feather-eating son-of-a-bitch: Eyes all red, plumage messed up, crazy tufts coming out of its face . . . anyone can tell this bird has problems just by looking at it.

You can find the Black-necked Grebe gobbling its own feathers and making its remorselessly repetitive, high-pitched duck-shrieks across freshwater lakes all over the world.

Uhhhch. Just talking about this bird makes me feel sick.

Bird Region: North America, Eurasia, Africa

BUMMR RATING

Eats own feathers:	*+35*
Probably neurotic:	*+5*
Seriously. **Eats bits of itself**:	*+173*
Gives you the heaves:	*213*

red eyes = crazy

blech-neck dweeb

Cactus Wretch

Campylorhynchus brunneicapillus

Common Name: Cactus Wren

These noisy little shits of the desert are commonly seen posturing with their wings and tails fanned out, eating spiders, scolding other birds, and hopping all over in the scrub brush like they're jacked up on speed.

Cactus Wrens build their distinctive nests in saguaro and cholla cacti, and by "distinctive," I mean ugly. Ever come across a fat wad of sticks and dirty plant fibers that looks like a hairy brown diaper stuck in a cactus? Then you've probably seen a Cactus Wren's nest.

If you have these birds nesting near your home, I am sorry, because their calls sound like someone trying to start an old Chrysler with an ignition problem. It's never going to start, but they just keep cranking it anyway.

It's the state bird of Arizona, which pretty much says it all.

Description: *Speckled brown with a long bill. You can't trust them, and they are way too fidgety.*

Bird Region: Central Mexico and southwestern United States

BUMMR RATING

Twitchiness:	-3
Trustworthy?:	-5
Nest aesthetics:	-70

Desirability in neighborhood: *No.*

Cactus Wretch

Rangy Poot

Fulica atra

Common Name: Eurasian Coot, Australian Coot, Common Coot

The Eurasian Coot's plumage is all black, which is surprisingly tasteful for a bird. They could almost be mistaken for ducks, except for the pale pinkish chicken beak and the small frontal shield that looks like a misshapen bald spot on their face.

"Whatever," you say. "A lot of birds look dumb."

Yes, I know, but take a look at those *feet*. They are, without a doubt, the creepiest-looking feet on a bird ever.

I mean it. Straight-up freak-feet. They're waaaaay too big for this bird. And worse yet, they are lobate feet,* which dials up the ick factor by about 900 percent.

Oh, and to top it all off, the feet are fucking blue. Yeah. Weird, fleshy, lobey, blue alien feet . . . *attached to bright yellow legs*! I mean, what the fuck. These birds do not belong on this planet.

Fun Fact: *These coots are quite vocal, making a variety of squeaks, squawks, and other unpleasant bird noises. Their nocturnal flight call is a high-pitched, trumpetlike honk, which sucks.*

Bird Region: Europe, Asia, Australia (and Africa and New Zealand, though they won't admit it)

---

*   I talk more about the different kinds of bird feet on page 173 of this book, in the section called "Bird Feet: Everything You Never Wanted to Know."

```
BUMMR RATING

Respectful plumage:        +1
Chicken beak:             Ha!
Shield-face:              -10
Night honking:            -20
Freak-feet:              900%
_____

Loveability (0-100):     -261
                   ("Hard no.")
```

hideous
lobate
← feet

Rangy poot

Ruddy Dick

Oxyura jamaicensis
Common Name: Ruddy Duck

These thick-necked brown ducks have blue bills and hold their tails upright, like they are better than other ducks. *(Fact: They're not.)*

Males are very aggressive during breeding season. They have an obnoxiously cocky attitude, probably because they have long penises compared to other ducks—Ruddy Duck dongs can measure nearly 10 inches (25 centimeters), which is more than half their body length. It's an absolute horror show, but it makes them all think they're god's gift to female ducks.

Anyway, the males try to attract mates by slapping their big blue bills against their fat duck necks to make bubbles in the water.

Ugh. Come and get it, ladies.

> **Description:** *I feel like we already know WAY more than we ever wanted to about this duck's physical attributes.*

Bird Region: The Americas, England (now spreading to Europe, which is alarming)

ruddy ~~dick~~ dick

warning:
do not look below
the waterline

```
BUMMR RATING

Aggressiveness:                         +5
Neck slapping:                          +3
Lame come-ons:                          +7
Proud of giant wang:                   +82
_____

Total grossness:                       +97
```

What-a-cock

Gallicrex cinerea

Common Name: Watercock

This dumb-looking bastard is a member of the rail family, Rallidae.

A ground-dwelling marsh bird, the Watercock can be found plucking insects and fish out of wetland mud across much of southern and eastern Asia, as well as Malaysia, the Philippines, and even some parts of Indonesia.

Its plumage is a nearly uniform charcoal gray, which is whatever, but its bright yellow feet are so ludicrously oversized that they look like they were borrowed from a clown.

Gallicrex cinerea has also evolved a distinctive red facial shield—this extended plate makes the bird's face look like it was designed for bashing open locked doors, but forget about it. The Watercock is actually much too lightweight and flimsy to be used effectively as a battering ram, rendering the bird useless.

Identification: *Look for the thin, dark, low-slung chicken with a bright red bike helmet and yellow garden rakes for feet.*

Bird Region: All over southern Asia

BUMMR RATING

Simple plumage:	*+1*
Choice of headwear:	*-38*
Usefulness:	*None*

Bird value:	*-37*
	("No.")

What a
Cock

Fuck I Hate These Birds

Another Hummingbird

Minima dickwaddus

Common Name: Oh, look, it's another fucking hummingbird

Yeah, I just can't do it.

Aside from their colors, these hovering pricks are all the same: a bunch of high-strung, busy little assholes who think that "fiesty" is a desirable personality trait.

Get the fuck out of my yard. Next bird.

another ~~hummi~~
hummingbird

who cares

fuck it

not drawing any
more goddamned
hummingbirds

~~bread~~

~~cheese~~

~~eggs~~

~~brocol~~

Broccoli
noodles!!

dry cleaner

BUMMR RATING

Fiesty attitude!:	-37
Over it:	-100
Fun to have around:	-137

Bum Flasher

Toxostoma rufum

Common Name: Brown Thrasher

This big Brown Thrasher is a common sight in much of North America, ranging from southern Canada through nearly all of central and eastern United States.

Toxostoma rufum is part of the same family as the mockingbirds (Mimidae), and males sing a loud and seemingly endless series of doubled phrases that have no discernible beginning or end. These phrases mimic the songs of other birds, and any one of these mouthy sons-of-bitches can have a combined repertoire of over a thousand of them.

A thousand! That's a very large number, especially when you consider that birds can't even count.

Imagine some dumb brown asshole yelling at the top of his bird lungs, a thousand crazy nonsense phrases that sound like "FOUND A SEED, FOUND A SEED, ATE IT, ATE IT! CHUP, CHUP! THERE'S A NICE WORM, THERE'S A NICE WORM! KITTY, KITTY! HI THERE, HI THERE! HAW, HAW, HAW! WHERE'S MY KEYS? WHERE'S MY KEYS?" on and on, etc., etc., ad infinitum.[*]

I mean, goddamn, dude. SHUT UP, SHUT UP!

---

[*] If you don't speak Latin, *ad infinitum* means "for fucking ever."

bum
flasher

mouthy

Brown thrasher identification guide

Figuring out which little brown & buff spotty-breasted bird you are observing can be hard! Try consulting this chart:

Q: was it worth it?

(write your answer on a 3x5 card and keep it handy for whenever you consider wasting time trying to identify a nondescript, boring brown bird

Identification: *Warm reddish brown on top, with buff, brown-streaked underparts. When seen through a tangle of branches, the Brown Thrasher can be easy to mistake for the smaller but similar-looking Wood Thrush, or maybe a dog turd that somehow got caught in a tree.*

Bird Region: A little bit of Canada, but mostly just the eastern United States, thank god

```
BUMMR RATING

Good for laughs (turd-like appearance):      +1
Large repertoire of bullshit:            -1,000

Overall appeal:                            -999
```

Goddamned Cackling Goose

Branta hutchinsii

Common Name: Cackling Goose

At first glance this bird looks like a small Canada Goose with a short neck, but it's not.

At least, not anymore. The Cackling Goose was once considered a subspecies of *Branta canadensis*, but in 2004 the American Ornithologists' Union Committee on Classification and Nomenclature divided them into two distinct species, and this noisy bastard got promoted to *Branta hutchinsii*.

Gas was thrown on the goose-fire in 2007 when posthumously published work by noted waterfowl expert Dr. Harold C. Hanson suggested that Cackling Geese and Canada Geese should actually be divided into *six* species, with at least *two hundred subspecies*. You can imagine the uproar at *that* year's "Symposium of Serious Ornithologists":

"Two species is more than enough. Has been for the last twenty years!"

"Oh, pull your heads out of the sand!"

"Please! This Branta *business is getting out of control!"*

"We've got to face the goose facts!"

(The assembly erupts into a chaos of separate arguments. Insults are hurled. Shoving ensues. A Sibley Guide *is*

goddamned
Canada
goose.
↓

JUST
HONKS
↑

"Cackles"

Short neck

no
neck-
ring

white
neckring →

both
same
type of
nuisance,
basically

↑
goddamned Cackling
goose

Geese : Always mad about Something.

What is their problem?

→ Main Types of geese

Show-offs

- white goose
  "I'm so beautiful."

- Red-breast (whatever)

- Emperor goose

  thinks he's somebody

→ obnoxious bastards

- Canada geese – aggressive

- Cackling goose – cackles

- Embden goose – tall, mean
  (but good for dinner)

- Chinese goose – too loud

- African goose – too loud
  and too large

122

thrown as someone in a powdered wig pounds a gavel for order . . .)

Regardless of how many taxa the science community ultimately divides the *Branta* genus into, *Branta hutchinsii* is definitely the worst, because it has driven full-grown ornithologists to fight among themselves about how many kinds of geese there are when they should be pulling together as peers and using their combined knowledge and intellect to determine something useful about geese, like how to get them all to leave.

Two species or two hundred, at the end of the day, it's still the same obnoxious goose bastards flying around, honking and shitting all over our public parks.

Identification Tip: *Compared to the Canada Goose, Cackling Goose vocalizations are higher in pitch and sound more like deranged duck laughter, which is arguably more annoying than normal honking.*

Region: Northern Alaska, migrating up and down North America, even Mexico

```
BUMMR RATING

New Smaller Size!:                      +10
Scientifically divisive:                -10
No honking!:                            +10
Cackling, though:                       -72
Still shitting everywhere:             -125
```

```
Gooseness Index:                       187%
```

Great-tailed Fuckle

Quiscalus mexicanus

Common Name: Great-tailed Grackle, Mexican Grackle

Also known as the Mexican Grackle, these scrawny-looking motherfuckers sport absurdly long tails and have a highly varied repertoire of shrill whistles, irritating shrieks, dumb squeaks, and rusty-door-hinge sounds that will be employed to bother you.

Known for extremely diverse foraging habits, they can be found eating grains, berries, insects, larvae, bird eggs (or the occasional nestling), lizards, and trash.

Or, in my own personal experience, *your food*. They will just steal it right off your goddamn plate. You turn your head for *one* second to order a cocktail from the poolside waiter and BA-BING! Their beaks are right in your shit, the thieving fucks.

I mean, *the nerve*.

Description: *Males are iridescent black and can often be seen strutting around with their heads up in the air, but trust me, they are nothing special. When molting, they often look weirdly gaunt and tattered and could easily be mistaken for poorly taxidermied crows.*

Region: Midwestern and southwestern United States and all the way down through Panama. Year-round, too.

great-tailed
Fuckle

BUMMR RATING

Nerve:	*+10*
Strut:	*+3*
Larceny:	*+18*

Chance this bird will steal your fries: *92.7%*

Northern Pinhead

Anas acuta

Common Name: Northern Pintail

Whereas most ducks average around 20 inches from head to tail, the Northern Pintail can measure up to 30 inches in length, but only because it has a pretentiously long neck. Honestly, what kind of duck needs a neck this long? It's like this pinhead thinks he's a swan or something.

Imagine the classic tale "The Ugly Duckling" by Hans Christian Andersen—only, in this version, the ugly duckling doesn't mature into a beautiful swan. He just grows up to be a weird-necked duck that all the real swans try to avoid at waterfowl parties.

When they're not grifting off some poor farmer's grain fields, these pintails feed like all dabbling ducks, plunging their heads and the top half of their bodies below the surface of the water. With their extra-long necks, pintails can dabble deeper, which I guess would be a benefit if you wanted to eat gross pond weeds that normal ducks can't reach.

Identification: *They have bluish-gray bills. Males have brown heads, white throats and breasts, gray-and-white backs, and long tails that are held upright. Other than that, just look for the duck with the stupidly long neck.*

Bird Region: Broad distribution worldwide, from Canada to Mexico, and northern Eurasia to Africa and Asia

Northern pinhead

BUMMR RATING

Too much neck:	-30
Thinks he's some kind of swan:	-60

Duck likeability score:	-90

("Complete duckwad.")

Red-belly Wood-crapper

Melanerpes carolinus

Common Name: Red-bellied Woodpecker

The Red-bellied Woodpecker is . . . wait a second, have I done this woodpecker already? Honestly, I don't even know anymore. I am so fucking sick of woodpeckers. They all start to blur together because they're pretty much just minor variations on the same tedious, red-capped, black-and-white bird.

The Red-bellied Woodpecker has some red on its belly (hence the name), but who cares? You can almost never see a woodpecker's belly because they've always got it hugged up against a tree trunk while they hammer away with their stupid wood-pecking beak.

Like most woodpeckers, *M. carolinus* eats a lot of insects, but it is actually an omnivore that also eats berries, nuts, and sometimes even small fish or frogs.

Why do they do all that obnoxious tree-hammering for a few nasty grubs when they could just as easily eat some fruit, or maybe a nice, quiet fish?

I'll tell you why: It's because they are inconsiderate assholes.

Region: North America (eastern United States, like all the time)

red-belly
wood-crapper

tiny bit
of red

rest just
standard pecker

BUMMR RATING

Black and white!:	+0
Red somewhere:	+0
Repetitive . . . :	-50
Noise:	-400
Makes me happy?:	-450

129

Losers

Blundering Albatrash

Diomedea exulans
Common Name: Wandering Albatross

It is difficult to say where the Wandering Albatross lives because of all the wandering. *D. exulans* has circumpolar range, meaning they just fly perpetually around the globe over the Antarctic Ocean. They can live up to fifty years and spend the majority of their life in the air over open sea.

Averaging an incredible 10 feet, 2 inches (3.1 meters), their wingspan is the largest of any living bird on earth, and they can weigh as much as 12.7 kilograms (that's 28 goddamned pounds). They are terrible at lifting off, but once they do manage to get airborne, those huge wings let them glide *for days at a time* while they forage for fish, cephalopods, and jellyfish. Just thinking about it is depressing.

Circling the Antarctic up to three times annually, these albatross only visit land once every two years in order to mate on isolated islands. A pair produces just one large egg. Once fledged, the lone young albatross will leave the nest, not returning to land again *for nine to eleven years*, when they themselves mature and return to breed.

You may be tempted to feel sympathy for this colossal sad sack and its existential isolation, but fuck that, because they also trail deep-sea vessels to gorge on floating ship's refuse until they're too bloated to fly and can only bob around on the waves like great big feathered bags of trash.

Bird Region: The vast, cold, uncaring open ocean (Antarctic)

blundering
albatrash

BUMMR RATING

Loneliness: *-13.330*
Trash: *-57.001*
Self-respect: *+0.000*

Bird value: *-70.331*
             (seagull,
             but worse)

Japanese Green Woodfucker

Picus awokera
Common Name: Japanese Woodpecker, Japanese Green
Woodpecker

This little fucker is, more or less, exactly the same as the
European Green Woodpecker except that it's from Japan.
If it were a whisky, this would make it nine times more
expensive. Whether it's nine times better is a matter of
opinion, but since we're talking about a woodpecker, not
whisky, it's hard to imagine spending any of your hard-earned
coin, unless it were to bribe this bird to go away.

In some ways *Picus awokera* actually *is* superior to other
woodpeckers: First, it is endemic to Japan—this means that
most of the world doesn't have to put up with the headache
of its loudly shrieked "PYO! PYO! PYO! PYO!" calls. (If you
do live in Japan, I'm sorry that this bird is probably ruining it
for you, but that's out of my hands.)

Second, it has a green back. This is great news because
you have no idea how goddamn sick I am of regular-looking
woodpeckers. Drawing those difficult-to-differentiate
black-and-white fuckers over and over again . . . honestly, it
starts to make you want to bang your own head against a tree
a few thousand times.

Of course, while the Japanese woodpecker's green
plumage is a refreshing change for all of us, he still wears the
distinctive red cap that is so common among members of

Japanese
GREEN
woodfucker

135

Woodpecker Notes

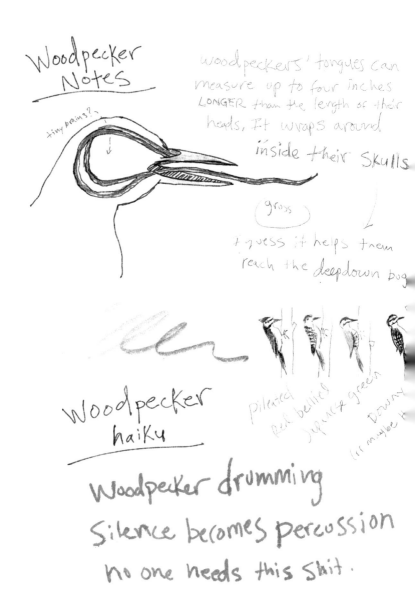

tiny brains?

woodpeckers' tongues can measure up to four inches LONGER than the length of their heads. It wraps around inside their skulls

gross

I guess it helps them reach the deepdown bug

pileated
red bellied
yellow & green
Downy (or maybe t

Woodpecker haiku

Woodpecker drumming
Silence becomes percussion
no one needs this shit.

the Picidae family. God, why do they all think it's so amazing? Hey, woodpeckers, I have a hot tip for you: The red hat is just tired and cliché at this point. Go home and change your look.

Whatever you think of this bird's sense of style, at the end of the day it's still a fucking woodpecker, and no amount of money or whisky is going to fix that.

Bird Region: Sorry, Japan, just you. Bad luck, I guess.

```
BUMMR RATING

Fresh color:                        +$20.00
Dated accessories:                   -$3.99
Still a woodpecker:                 -$49.99
_____

Suggested retail:                   -$33.98
                                (refund due)
```

Horn-dork

Eremophila alpestris

Common Name: Horned Lark, Shore Lark

Holy crap, this stupid lark is everywhere.

Actually, it's more like forty-two larks in six different clades. Regardless of how you count them, they are widespread in the northern hemisphere, which is another way of saying that they have infested the whole top half of the globe.

They can be found on posts, rocks, or any other low mound of dirt that they can sing from. Their song is a high-pitched tinkle of notes. It's a soft and weak tinkle, but it can last up to a solid minute, so if there are more than one of them around, the cumulative aggravation level can be off the charts.

In Europe, this member of the family Alaudidae is called a Shore Lark, because it is found in wintertime along the seashores. In North America, it is known as the Horned Lark, because it has horns and we call it like we see it.

Within their vast range, you will find these ground feeders running around everywhere from the mountains to the lowlands, all over farmlands, prairies, golf resorts, and just about any other open ground in between . . . There's no escaping this horned dipwad's long, tinkly, weak-ass song.

Bird Region: Practically the whole top half of the world (except Africa, which has its own lark problems)

horn-dork

BUMMR RATING

Chance of Spotting *E. alpestris*:   +99
Chance of Avoiding *E. alpestris*:   -02

Lark-free fun in North America: *Approaching 0%*

Mah Blah Blah Trogon

Harpactes fasciatus

Common Name: Malabar Trogon

The Malabar Trogon is a colorful but lazy tropical bastard who loiters quietly in the forests of Sri Lanka and the Indian peninsula.

Though these insectivores will sometimes descend to the forest floor for food, they much prefer the minimum-effort approach of foraging the bark of whatever tree they already happen to be loafing in. They sometimes just hang upside down from their perch if they think they can reach a bug without having to leave the branch.

Mating pairs will excavate a nest hole in a rotting tree because the soft wood is easy to dig out with their bills. In spite of this, it still takes them a month to finish a hole. Even then, they don't bother to line it—they just leave a bunch of wood chips in the bottom and call it good.

The female lays a single pair of eggs, taking a two-day break in between them. She feeds the hatchlings (which is sort of the bare minimum when it comes to bird parenting) but doesn't even bother to clean their waste out of the nest hole. Juveniles expect to be fed by their mother for up to six months after they leave the nest.

Jesus, what a lazy-ass bird.

Bird Region: India and Sri Lanka

mah blah blah
trogon

what a
lazy fuck

BUMMR RATING

Hardworking?:   *+0*
Sensible attire?:   *+0*
Keeps a clean house?:   *No.*

Bird-Personality Type: *Lazy fuck*

Northern Brown Creepy

Apteryx mantelli

Common Name: North Island Brown Kiwi

This is one weird-looking bird. Imagine a pouf-ball standing about 15 inches (40 centimeters) tall on ungainly chicken legs, tail-less and covered in brownish, spiky-looking feathers. They look like no-budget aliens from a tacky 1960s sci-fi movie.

To make matters worse for this hideous bird, it has tiny, black, beady eyes set on what appears to be a mouse's head. The mouse head terminates in a long, proboscis-like bill, which the kiwis poke in the dirt, foraging for invertebrates to eat.

It is the most common kiwi remaining, but they are listed as "vulnerable" by the International Union for Conservation of Nature, which is not surprising because kiwis are weak—they are slower than dogs and cats, plus they lack the ability to fly, which, let's face it, is a pretty significant deficiency for a small, plump, convenient meal on short legs. Amazingly, they can live up to forty years, though why they would want to is beyond explanation.

The North Island Brown Kiwi's song is a sort of mournful wail that is repeated again and again—as would be yours, if you were one of these cursed, hairy-looking bastards.

Bird Region: New Zealand, but just the northern part

Northern
brown creepy

Short-
weak
weird
(knows *4*)

BUMMR RATING

Looks:	*-10*
Weirdness:	*-18*
Weakness:	*-23*
Cursed:	*-10*

| Total usefulness as a bird: | *-61* |

Xinjiang Clown Jay

Podoces biddulphi

Common Name: Xinjiang Ground Jay

Endemic to China, this small, black-and-white-winged corvid is dressed in a suit of pale brown feathers. Its thin, sharp beak curves downward into a perpetual frown, from underneath which a black "mustache" swoops up dramatically toward its black cap.

Taken all together, this makes the jay look a lot like the churlish villain in a nineteenth-century melodrama—one who would definitely kidnap the beautiful heroine and attempt to force her into marriage in spite of her devotion to her one true love, the handsome and virtuous hero of the story (who, let's face it, is a bit of a Goody Two-shoes and ought to be taken down a notch on the grounds of his over-earnest personality alone).

But alas, the Xinjiang Ground Jay is just another typical fucking bird. Instead of twirling his mustache and realizing his dastardly plans, he spends his life making rapid, annoying, high-pitched chattering calls, and running around the grassy desert areas of northwest China, trying to chase down bugs to eat.

What a goddamn waste of villainous potential.

Bird Region: Xinjiang, China

BUMMR RATING

Sweet mustache!:	+3
Looks old-time villain-y!:	+25
Just does bird shit:	-800

Squandered opportunity?: *Huge.*

Xinjiang
Clown Jay

MWAH
HAH
HAH

Dollar Nerd

Eurystomus orientalis

Common Name: Dollarbird, Oriental Dollarbird

The Dollarbird belongs to a family of Old World birds known as "rollers" because of their daring displays of high-speed arial acrobatics, a behavior that clearly stems from a compulsive need to be the center of attention.

Like most rollers, *E. orientalis* is small and stocky, flat headed, and has a slightly hooked beak. Being unattractive creates a deep-seated sense of inadequacy that fuels its unquenchable craving for external validation.

Predictably, these flying attention-seekers feel compelled to sport unnecessarily flashy plumage in order to prove to themselves that they are not as dull and ugly as they feel. But their glossy blackish-brown heads, brilliant blue throats, deep, gemlike greenish-blue backs, and pale blue underparts cannot disguise the fact that they feel worthless inside.

The name *Dollarbird* comes from the two bright white patches visible on the undersides of the wings, which are called dollars, and also likely reflect subconscious fears about their value as birds.

When not desperately trying to impress everyone, this sad little bird can be found perched alone on branches in high trees telling itself that it is popular.

Bird Region: All over the place, southern Himalayas down through much of Asia, Japan, parts of India, and Australia

dollar nerd

"dollars"

BUMMR RATING

Insecurity:	*-20*
Overcompensation (plumage):	*-8*
Overcompensation (rolling):	*-10*
Named after money:	*+$1*
Actual worth:	*-37*

Shoe-face Dork

Balaeniceps rex
Common Name: Shoe-billed Stork, Shoebill, Whale-headed
Stork, Whalebill

The Shoebill is a long-legged wading bird found in the fresh-water swamps of central Africa.

In addition to Shoebill, it has a number of other common names: Shoe-billed Stork, Whalebill, Whale-headed Stork . . . this bird has never been called a name that doesn't sound like an insult.

Its great big shoe-like bill can measure nearly 9 inches (24 centimeters). The upper mandible ends in a downturned spike. It makes for a hideous face, but it's probably useful for hunting, and it will eat just about any wetland vertebrate it can get that big, horrible bill around. This includes frogs and snakes, and its favorite prey of all, the lungfish.

Sure, go ahead. Gobble down some big, weird, slippery fish with lungs and a face not even a mother could love. No one is going to think any less of you than they already do.

Fun Fact: They were formerly considered relatives of storks, but genetic testing has recently placed B. rex in the order of Pelecaniformes, much to the bitter embarrassment of pelicans, herons, and bitterns everywhere.

Bird Region: Limited to Central Africa, thank god

BUMMR RATING

Feet:	*-3*
Face:	*-50*
Diet:	*Lungfish*

Bird appeal: *-106*
("Barf.")

shoe-face
dork

big face
big feet
bad brain

Bad-cheeks Cordonbleu

Uraeginthus bengalus

Common Name: Red-cheeked Cordonbleu

Holy shit, this bird looks like it put on its makeup drunk in a gas station restroom.

The Red-cheeked Cordonbleu is a small, seed-eating waxbill common across western, central, and eastern Africa, and can be found in dry grasslands or in open terrain around human-inhabited areas.

The male has brown upperparts and belly, bright blue chest and tail, and clownish magenta patches on his cheeks—a brazenly loud color combo. (The female doesn't have these face markings; her plumage tends toward brown, making her appearance bearable, if not her choice of mates.)

Cordonbleus belong to the family Estrildidae, and some scientists believe them to be part of a species complex* with the Blue Waxbill, a bird that looks almost identical, except without the tawdry cheek patches.

So why is this bird called the Red-cheeked Cordonbleu when it probably should have been called the Too-much-rouge Waxbill? Who the hell knows.

---

* *Species complex* is a term used by scientists to describe a group of two or more "closely related" species so similar in appearance that it is uncertain where one species begins and the other ends. It may be unclear if there are multiple species under one name, or how exactly they are related. To make matters worse, the horny bastards may confuse things by interbreeding. (I mean the species, not the scientists.)

Bad-cheeks
cordonbleu

The red-cheeked cordonbleu was first described in 1760 by Mathurin Jacques Brisson in Ornithologie Brisson. If he ever ate one is still unknown...

artist's interpretation of 18th century French naturalist Mathurin Jacques Brisson

The phrase *cordon bleu* comes from the term for the blue ribbons worn by an order of knights under King Henry III (who were known for decadent feasts), and it is now synonymous with culinary excellence. I can't prove it, but I'm guessing this bird was named by an eighteenth-century French naturalist who secretly ate one.

Bird Region: Right across the middle of Africa

```
BUMMR RATING

Personal appearance:                    Garish
Questionable lineage:                      -80
The French connection:                      -5
Might be delicious:                         +1
_____

Tastefulness level:                          F
_____

Recommendation: Complete makeover
```

Uncomely Wood Pudgeon

Columba palumbus

Common Name: Common Wood Pigeon, Wood Pigeon

Columba palumbus—this bird's scientific name sounds like a sarcastic comment you'd make about an inept workmate.

"Gee-whiz, now that Detective *Columba Palumbus* is on the case, I'm sure *The Mystery of How to Change the Printer Toner* will be solved in no time."

In addition to being useless in the workplace, this big, fat, dopey pigeon is useless across most of Europe as well.

It has a a regular-size gray pigeon head attached to a large, bulky body, and plumage the color of brown, but with equal parts boring and dreary mixed in.

Their diet is mostly vegetarian: berries, grains, cabbage, and anything else the crop-thieving buttholes can steal from a farmer in the countryside, though some prefer city living, where they can skulk in hedges and pilfer food scraps instead.

While its behavior is mostly "standard pigeon" (loitering, cooing, looking stupid), this hapless clod is also known for its total lack of awareness, frequently blundering out of bushes like a graceless community theater actor who has tripped on a sandbag and stumbled onstage during the wrong scene.

What a fucking *palumbus*.

Bird Region: Europe, parts of western Asia, and Africa, I guess

BUMMR RATING

Pigeon:	+100
Body, too big:	+25
Color: *"browring"*	+25
Stage presence:	-3
Pigeon?:	176%

uncomely
wood
pudgeon

BIRD
ASSESSMENT
DUMBFUCK
BIRD
ASSESSMENT

The Horror. The Horror.

Andean Cockhead

Rupicola peruvianus

Common Name: Andean Cock-of-the-rock

Rupicola peruvianus lives in the forested ravines of the Andes mountain range, from Venezuela all the way down through Bolivia.

This large tropical passerine has a big, bulbous head shaped like, uh . . .

The average male Cock-of-the-rock is about 12 inches in length and, wow, this description is not getting any easier. He has black-and-gray wings and a thick red-orange body and head. The feathers of his rounded crest obscure his beak, making him look like, I'll just say it, a great big swollen red knob.

There's no shame in being fascinated by a bird like this. It's normal to be curious, even if you're not attracted to them. Birds, I mean. I hate birds, but I can't take my eyes off this one. This is starting to feel uncomfortable, isn't it?

Identification Tip: *Having no crest and bearing only non-descript reddish-brown plumage, females could almost be mistaken for some kind of drab pigeon, and I imagine they frequently wish they would be.*

Bird Region: Popping up in Venezuela, Colombia, Ecuador, Peru, and Bolivia

BUMMR RATING

Crest hides face: *+10*
Overall cock-ness: *-130*

───────────────────────────

Bird rating: *TV-MA*
 (mature audiences only)

Andean Cockhead

Fire Kook

Milvus migrans
Common Name: Black Kite, Fire Kite

Known as the Black Kite, this dark, nondescript, medium-size raptor looks boring, but he is a total psychopath.

They are sometimes referred to as "Fire Kites" because of their curious habit of always turning up where there is an active wildfire. They circle the rising smoke, scanning for rodents trying to escape the flames, then swoop down and snatch them up in their talons, just as the victim thinks it's about to reach safety. Fire Kites are total heartless bastards.

"So what?" you say. "All raptors are heartless bastards."

You're right about that, but *M. migrans* takes the dickery to a whole new level: They actually *start* the fires, too.

Yes, you heard me right. This flying pyromaniac is known to pick up burning material from one fire, then take it somewhere else, and drop it into some nice dry grass to burn down some more real estate.

Some experts believe they do this to be the first on the scene of a fire, thus getting the jump on their competition for prey. Sure, or maybe these sick fucks just like to watch the flames before they kill, because that all sounds like the work of a homicidal arsonist to me. If you spot one of these kites in your area, my advice is to invest in a good fire extinguisher.

Bird Region: Africa, Asia, Europe, Australia, wherever they can watch some shit burn

Fire Kook

BIRD BRAND MATCHES

BUMMR RATING

Has learned to
use fire: +10
Uses fire for evil: -10
Pyromaniac: -25
Danger to life and
property: -75

Recommendation: Immediate incarceration

Great Regret

Ardea alba

Common Name: Great Egret, Great White Egret, Common Egret

The Great Egret is a large white heron distributed throughout most of the world, with populations breeding and migrating in North and South America, Eurasia, and Africa.

They are typically found foraging in wetlands and shallow waters, mostly eating fish and frogs, though sometimes they eat small mammals like mice (which, honestly, seems kind of wrong for a wading bird).

Slightly smaller than the Great Blue Heron, *Ardea alba* is pure white. During the breeding season, adults develop a patch of neon green skin around their eyes and grow long, billowy plumes called aigrettes,* which they flounce around in to get attention.

So far, so what, right?

Well, here's the terrifying part: Nestlings frequently practice siblicide. Siblicide is when the larger, *evil* sibling kills the smaller, *good* one, usually by pecking them to death with its long, sharp, evil beak. Experts say this behavior is probably an evolutionary strategy allowing the strongest offspring to

---

* These delicate plumes were so popular for women's hats in the late nineteenth and early twentieth centuries that Great Egrets were overhunted in North America, slaughtered nearly to extinction for haute couture, which, by the way, should not be a surprise to anyone familiar with the fashion industry. Alarmed by the carnage, conservation groups in the early 1900s organized boycotts of feathered clothing and introduced legislation that banned plume hunting. Today the Great Egret is thriving, and its population and range seems to be expanding. Nice work, hippies.

stabby
beak
killing
(stabbings)

aigrettes
(dancing
wings)

Great Regret

163

Nigel, be a good chap and go
kill a fuckload of majestic birds,
will you? I need a new hat.

• All the rage in Paris!
• Look like you have a bird on your head!

benefit solely from limited food provided by parents in times when food is scarce.

Nice theory, experts, but my guess is these evil creeps just hatch from the egg already filled with sibling jealousy and a cold-blooded willingness to murder.

Bird Region: They're all over the place, man.

BUMMR RATING

Appearance of respectability:	+2
Murders own family members:	-10
Maybe it's just nature's way?:	+10
No, that's fucked up:	-99
Is this bird a good person?:	-97
	(No.)

Crowned Evil (The King of Murder)

Stephanoaetus coronatus
Common Name: Crowned Eagle, African Crowned Eagle, Crowned Hawk–Eagle

Considered the most powerful raptor in Africa, this lethal bastard inhabits sub-Saharan woodlands and forests. Its range extends in a southwestward diagonal stripe across the continent, from Senegal through Tanzania, and down through Mozambique and South Africa.

Crowned Eagles have long legs and strong, lengthy talons, which they use for impaling their prey when they strike. However, if body-puncturing doesn't do the trick, they will also happily employ spine-breaking and/or skull-crushing as a means of dispatch for anyone unlucky enough to be on the business end of their sadistic murder-feet.

Nearly all of their diet is made up of mammals. Their victims are primarily rock hyrax (sometimes called rock rabbits or dassie) but also small hoofed animals (like mouse-deer and antelopes) and small primates. Yes, you heard that right: This feathered terror nonchalantly hunts and kills goddamn *antelopes and monkeys*.

Oh, and here's a bird-watching pro tip for you: Don't ever, ever, *ever* go near one of their nests, because these psychos will not even hesitate to assault you. Believe me, that's a fight you want to avoid, because they're not afraid of you and they don't give a shit.

Crowned
EVIL

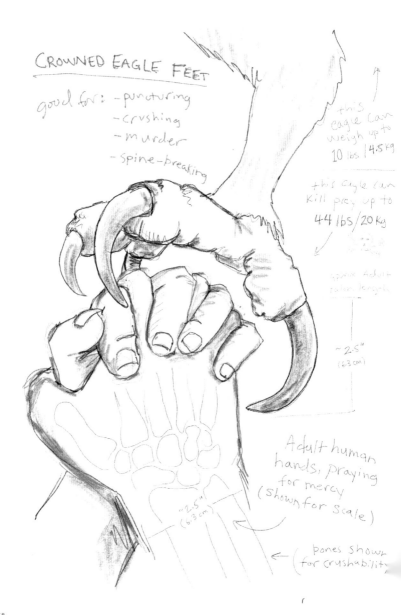

CROWNED EAGLE FEET

good for: - puncturing
- crushing
- murder
- spine-breaking

this eagle can weigh up to 10 lbs / 4.5 kg

this eagle can kill prey up to 44 lbs / 20 kg

approx Adult talon length

~ 2.5"
(6.3 cm)

Adult human hands, praying for mercy
(shown for scale)

~ 2.5"
(6.3 cm)

bones shown
(for crushability

It should probably be mentioned that the Crowned Eagle *is not* the only bird who will attack humans in defense of their nests, but it *is* the only bird known to *hunt human children as prey.*

Holy fuck, what a monster.

Bird Region: Sub-Saharan Africa

```
BUMMR RATING

Tough-looking:                              +10
Bloodthirst:                               -13
Compassion:                               +0.0
Spine-breaking:                            -79
Hunts monkeys, babies:                  -1,000
_____

Good person?:                           -1,082
                                 ("Pure evil.")
```

Section 3:

And Another Thing . . .

Bird Feet:

Everything You Never Wanted to Know

Bird feet are gross, but also there are a surprising number of toe configurations found in different species.

Why do birds come with so many different types of feet?

Scientists believe that birds evolved different toe configurations as adaptations to help them acquire the foods they eat or to better navigate the physical environments in their respective habitats. In other words, their feet are adapted to what they do and where they do it. I mean, obviously, anything else would be stupid, even for a bird.

For example, imagine a chickadee with duck feet. Ha ha, he looks so dumb, but also that chickadee would have a very difficult time trying to grasp on to the small branches where they perch to eat berries and insects.

Now imagine a duck with the feet of a chickadee. First of all, they would be laughably small feet for a duck. Also, chickadee feet are not webbed, so the ducks wouldn't be able to paddle with them at all. It would be chaos. Confused ducks drifting around lakes willy-nilly, waiting helplessly for something edible to drift within reach of their bills, all while crashing into each other like rudderless boats. Ha ha, boy, I'd pay to see that.

Anyway, ducks obviously evolved their big, awkward webbed feet so that they could propel themselves through the water. It was either that or be the small-footed laughingstock of every lake, pond, and estuary.

By the same token, woodpeckers' feet are adapted to their own special requirements—they have two toes forward and two toes back, which is perfect for hanging on to vertical tree trunks while they drive everyone crazy with their incessant wood pecking.

While we know that birds evolved a wide variety of foot types specialized for different lifestyles, one question scientists have not yet answered about them is "Why did bird feet all evolve to be so goddamn nasty looking?"

Seriously. They all look like gross little skeleton claws that are barely covered in dried-out skin. I mean, really. If you are going to have toes like that, do us all a favor and put some fucking socks on.

On the following pages is a list of the different bird toes. If it creeps you out like it does me, you don't have to look at it.

In spite of what you've seen in the bad drawings on people's refrigerators, nearly all birds have four toes, not three. That said, there are a few exceptions: Rheas and emus have three toes; ostriches have only two incredibly ugly toes. *(Fun fact: They can kick you to death with those big ugly toes, so don't laugh at them in front of the Ostrich.)*

The first toe on a bird's foot is called the hallux. In fact, humans have a hallux, too—it's your big toe! A bird's big toe faces backward, which I think we can all agree is messed up.

SKELETON FEET

Sometimes called unwebbed feet, these mostly belong to the kinds of birds that don't spend much time swimming.

Anisodactyl

These are your basic model, no-frills bird feet. Most passerines have them because they are cheap and good for perching. You can also walk on them if you are too lazy to fly for some reason.

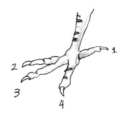

Believe it or not, hawks and eagles also have this toe configuration, but most people don't notice because theirs are much more muscular and are often obscured by the mangled bodies of their unlucky victims.

Zygodactyl

This popular style of foot has toes 1 and 4 pointing backward, and toes 2 and 3 pointing forward. How that makes sense is anyone's guess,

but this configuration is still found on many different birds. Woodpeckers like them because two toes backward provide extra stability while you hold on to trees and hammer your face into the trunk. Parrots use them to hold pieces of fruit while they eat, even though eating with your feet is disgusting.

Heterodactyl

This is basically just zygodactyl, but with the toes switched up. Only trogons have this type of foot, and it's stupid.

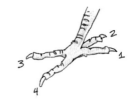

Semizygodactyl

Remember anisodactyl and zygodactyl? Some birds, like osprey and owls, can rotate toe 4 from front to back. This means they can transform from anisodactyl to

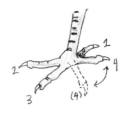

zygodactyl feet whenever they feel like it, which probably annoys the living hell out of the other birds.

"Check it out, losers: anisodactyl... zygodactyl... anisodactyl... zygodactyl..."

Owls enjoy using zygodactyl mode because it's very good for snatching terrified mice off the ground and then carrying them away into the night to be torn limb from limb and devoured.

Pamprodactyl

The two front toes (2 and 3) can rotate *backward*, and the two back toes (1 and 4) can rotate *forward*, and now we've got goddamn bird toes going all over everywhere like there are no rules anymore.

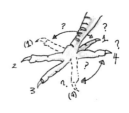

Syndactyl

Syndactyl is basically just aniso-dactyl, except fucked up because toes 2 and 3 are *partially fused.* Kingfishers have this type of foot. They seem to get by okay in life,

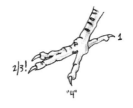

but only because their job is limited to dropping out of trees and flying face-first into the water. Birds with fused syndactyl toes are not technically considered malformed, but let's be honest, no one wants to see their weird, birdy goblin-feet.

WEBBED FEET

Birds who spend a lot of time in the water often have webbing between their toes for swimming, paddling, or otherwise moving themselves around. It may be practical, but frankly it looks much better on frogs. It should be noted that not all birds with webbed feet actually swim—some just use them to schlep around on soft mud or snow.

Palmate

This is your standard-issue toe webbing, and it spans most of the area between the front toes. You'll see this setup on swans, geese, ducks, gulls, terns . . . you name it. Efficient for pushing yourself around in the water, but you look like an idiot walking around on dry land.

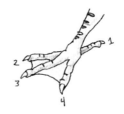

Semipalmate

This is similar to palmate, but the webbing is thinner and does not cover as much area. It is common to many shorebirds and water-adjacent birds (like sandpipers, 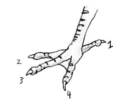 plovers, and herons) who need to get around in wet environments but don't want the embarrassment of looking like a duck.

Totipalmate

Some water birds, like cormorants and pelicans, have webbing between *all four toes*, making them look like they are walking around on old 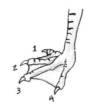 stretched-out baseball mitts. This is why these birds rarely take their feet out of the water if anyone else might see them.

Lobate

A lot of grebes and coots have this style of feet. For my money, lobate are the grossest bird feet of all; they combine the worst of both worlds, being neither skeleton feet nor webbed feet, but having 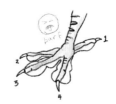 fleshy "lobes" that provide expanded surface for swimming or walking in mud. You can just imagine the awful, squishy, sucking sound they must make when these birds trudge around in the muck. Ugh. I just gave myself the shudders.

chickadees did not evolve
duck feet because:

A. would always
   be falling
   out of trees

B. laughed at
   by other birds

C. look stupid
   when flying

D. evolutionary
   pressures   technically correct
                                (Probably true)
E.   ALL of the above

F. peer pressure

                            You can't tell me
                            it wouldn't have been
                            fun to see, though.

Identifying a Bird's Primary Character Defect

Birds are terrible at many things, but one area they are particularly bad at is self-assessment. Most people would agree, it's healthy to periodically evaluate our own choices and habits in order to identify areas where there is an opportunity for personal growth, but I have never seen a bird do this.

As frustrating as it may be, we can't really blame the birds; they don't have the strength of character required to take a hard look inward, much less the courage to be honest with themselves about their own shortcomings. For birds, there is little chance of personal growth, but that doesn't have to stop us from assessing and evaluating their deep and numerous personality flaws for them.

It would be unfair to expect the average reader to follow my rigorous scientific methods or to produce the level of detailed analysis that I have in my ongoing ornithological work, but there is no reason you can't apply the basic principles in order to better understand the failings of the birds in your life.

The following is a brief primer and a checklist for identifying any bird's primary character defects.

Identify accomplishments.

As you begin this bird assessment, begin with the bird's accomplishments. Consider the bird's personal and professional goals, and how they have performed against them this year. This is likely to be a difficult task, as few birds bother to define goals for themselves, and therefore rarely accomplish anything of note.

Identify patterns.

If you study a bird long enough, you will begin to notice certain repeated behaviors or tendencies. Some of these behaviors are the product of millions of years of adaptation in order to survive and reproduce successfully in their environments. But in many cases, repeated tendencies point to a significant underlying personality issue. The list on the opposite page is not exhaustive, but it will get you thinking in the right direction.

BEHAVIOR	ISSUE
Not listening actively	Impatience
Chattering/squawking when others are speaking	Self-absorption
Just flies away when others are speaking	Lack of manners
Loud/persistent morning song	Narcissism
Scolding/swooping	Anger issues
Stealing	Lack of morals
Mocking or mimicking other species	Low empathy
Overly boisterous and energetic/can't sit still	Drug problem
Cheerful at inappropriate times	Lack of emotional intelligence
Can't stop spilling seeds out of feeder	Lack of self-control
Trespassing on others' property	Boundary issues
Defecating on others' property	Complete asshole
Just flitting around all the time	Stupidity

Ask hard questions.

I have designed the following survey to help you take an objective look at a bird's personality and ask some hard questions. The process of contemplating each question and answering it may help you to come to a better understanding of this bird.

1. **What traits do I most dislike in this bird?** List the three that bother you most.

2. **Are these traits reflected in the personalities of any people I know?** What is that person's problem? Is it possible that this bird has the same issues?

3. **What are this bird's apparent weaknesses?** List them all. If you are able to think of a strength, I guess you can write that down, too, but don't spend too much time racking your brain for something nice to say.

4. **How self-aware is this bird?**

5. **Has there ever been an occasion when this bird lost its temper and scolded you or someone you know?** List each incident and note why it was undeserved.

6. **Has this bird done something that it should be ashamed of?** Scientists believe that birds are born without a shame gland, but that is no excuse. List any shameful actions you are aware of.

7. **Does this bird ever sabotage your happiness?** Describe how this bird sabotages your happiness. Is it possible that this bird somehow thrives on drama or conflict in your life? (Yes, it is.)

8. **To what extent has this bird taken responsibility for the problems they create?**

9. **What behaviors or physical attributes would you try to hide from the world if you were this bird?**

10. **Does this bird exhibit any contradictory behaviors?** Why don't these contradictions bother them?

Finally, there are no right or wrong answers. The most important part of this process is honesty. Remember, if you're not honest with the bird, you're not helping anyone.

Emotional Tools for Bird-watchers

If you are inexperienced with bird-watching, you might imagine that it must involve all the challenges and difficulties of the great outdoors, such as traversing difficult terrain, unpredictable weather, and all that dirt. But that does not always have to be the case.

First of all, birds live everywhere, so they can be readily studied not only in fields and forests but also in urban and suburban environments like parks, gardens, or even from the comfort of your own home, provided your own home has windows.

Additionally, with a little planning plus the right shoes and outerwear, even a hike in the field need not be unpleasant. It can actually be an agreeable way to connect with nature, bugs notwithstanding.

In spite of all this, bird-watching cannot really be considered a relaxing outdoor hobby, because the whole goddamn thing is centered around birds, who are a major cause of irritation in and of themselves. Sadly, there is little we can do about this, since most birds won't listen to anyone, and those that will can't be reasoned with. Trust me, I have tried.

Maybe, like me, you study birds in a professional capacity. Or perhaps you are a masochist, or the kind of person who, for some incomprehensible reason, thinks that birding is meant to be "fun."

Whatever the reason, if you are unable or unwilling to avoid avians altogether, you may still benefit from the following suggestions for how to keep yourself centered while weathering the inevitable emotional disturbance of spending your time watching birds.

Track your stressors.

By *stressors* I mean birds, obviously.

Many bird enthusiasts keep a bird journal. If you don't keep one, I highly recommend it! You can use it to identify the birds you see and which ones create the most stress for you.

Note the time and place that you come across those birds, and write down your thoughts and feelings about the encounter. What did this little fucker do? How did you react? Did you raise your voice at the bird? Did you make rude hand gestures? Did you wish you could hide in your bathroom and drink mini bottles of tequila in the dark until the bird went away?

Many mental health professionals believe that self-documenting like this can help you discern patterns in your stressors and how you react to them. What good that is, I have no idea. I guess at least later there will be a written record for the psychiatrist.

Don't take it personally.

It can be very frustrating when the birds don't cooperate with your plans or schedule. Let's say, for example, you travel to a location in the field to observe birds of some particular species, and you hope to capture a few good photos while you're there. So you spend the whole morning trekking to this perfect spot and then carefully position yourself in some bushes that will act as a natural blind.

Now it's hours later. Hours squatting in those bushes. Camera in hand, just squatting there, so quiet, scarcely breathing, trying to swat a cloud of gnats away from your face without making any sudden movements that might frighten off a bird . . . You're a bit too warm, hungry now, legs cramped, bladder full, sweat trickling down your spine, still slow-motion bug-swatting (which not only looks foolish but is completely ineffective against gnats), and, wow, it's getting really warm out now, should you put the camera down and take off your fleece? Never mind, the sweat has already trickled down the small of your back, made it past your beltline, and is now illegally crossing the border into Buttsylvania. It is around this time that you realize the birds you came to photograph have not even bothered to show up . . .

Emotionally, this feels a lot like sitting alone in a restaurant, realizing you've been stood up for a date, after you spent all day trying on different outfits and practicing your genuinely-fascinated-by-this-story face in the mirror while trying to fix your hopeless hair so that it looks devil-may-care while at the same time forcing that goddamn cowlick to lie down and stay where it belongs. Being ghosted by birds after you have invested so much time, effort, and anticipation can be truly crushing.

Grounding Exercise: *Stand up straight. Inhale deeply. Hold it for a moment, and then let it out slowly. Acknowledge your feelings of being let down. Remind yourself that this is just part of dating. I mean, birding.*

Now say to yourself, "There is no reason to be angry or hurt. This is not personal. It's not about me."

(In my experience that's a lie. It most definitely is personal. But this is still a good technique to help yourself feel better in the moment. At least it will get you home, where you can put on sweatpants and open a bottle of wine. Remember, those birds did not deserve your attention, and they are the ones who are missing out.)

Establish boundaries.

Ha ha, birds don't have personal boundaries and they don't respect anyone else's, so just forget about this one. Establishing healthy boundaries with in-laws and your boss is hard enough, so just focus on that. You don't stand a chance with birds.

Take time to recharge.

Bird-watching, birding, twitching—whatever you call it, it can become a bit of an obsession for some people. Between studying field guides, attending club events, going on bird outings, and actually observing the birds, it's easy to quickly become burned out.

It's necessary for us to find ways to relax, recharge our batteries, and return to pre-bird stress levels, so that we can function normally around our friends and family. At least normally enough that they don't feel inclined to constantly point out our nervous ticks, twitching eyelid, and unusual irritability.

There are many healthy ways to take a break from thinking about birds, like meditation, working out at the gym, or knitting . . . but how you disconnect and spend time focused on bird-free activities really comes down to whatever works best for you.

The important thing is that you get away from the birds for a while and find an activity that allows you to restore yourself and bank emotional strength for when they find you again—*they* meaning the birds, but then maybe you also need a break from your family, not judging. (Pro tip: bathroom mini tequilas.)

Section 4:

Oh, You Wanted a Geographical Index?

Birds exist all over the goddamn world. There's nothing we can do about it at this point, so we might as well just accept it and get on with our lives.

This book includes many different birds from around the globe, which I have organized according to their general effect on my nerves. And while I believe this system will be easy and relatable enough for modern-day bird enthusiasts, I acknowledge that this is a nontraditional structure for bird guides. If you are an ornithologist, zoogeographer, or just some fusty old bird-watcher who dislikes new things, I apologize for the irregularity of this approach. But also, deal with it, because it's not all about you.

However, I am nothing if not generous and empathetic to my readers—so I have included the following index of birds, organized by geographic region. You're welcome.

You may notice that many species in the index are listed in more than one region, and some may not be listed in all the regions that you think they should—this is because birds, having no respect for indexing systems, migrate wherever they please, and, by the way, that's why I didn't organize this book by region in the first place.

Here's Your Goddamn Index

North America

South America

Everywhere Else (Oceania)

Undecided

(Still Circling . . .)

References

BOOKS AND ARTICLES

Bent, Arthur Cleveland. "Life Histories of North American Flycatchers, Larks, Swallows, and Their Allies. Order Passeriformes (Families Cotingidae, Tyrannidae, Alaudidae, and Hirundinidae)." *Bulletin of the United States National Museum* 179 (1942): 438–57. https://doi.org/10.5479/si.03629236.179.i.

Cornell Lab of Ornithology. "Voices: Common Nighthawk." May 24, 2010. YouTube video, 2:40. https://www.youtube.com/watch?v=9qpsyjmda5Q.

Kaufman, Kenn, and Kimberly Kaufman. "Where Do Migratory Birds Spend the Winter?" *Birds and Blooms*, March 26, 2024. https://www.birdsandblooms.com/travel/birding-hotspots/where-do-migrating-birds-spend-the-winter/.

Milius, Susan. "Duck Penis Length Depends on Other Guys." *Wired*, August 2, 2018. https://www.wired.com/2010/08/duck-penises/.

Miller, John MacNeill. "Is It Really So Wrong to Kill a Mockingbird?" The Millions, July 21, 2016. https://themillions.com/2016/07/really-wrong-kill-mockingbird.html.

Ozaki, Yei Theodora. "Momotaro, or the Story of the Son of a Peach." In *Japanese Fairy Tales*. Lit2Go edition, 1908. https://etc.usf.edu/lit2go/72/japanese-fairy-tales/4845/momotaro-or-the-story-of-the-son-of-a-peach/.

Scopel, Lauren. "Diomedea exulans (Wandering Albatross)." Animal Diversity Web, 2007. https://animaldiversity.org/accounts/Diomedea_exulans/.

Stanisław, Serf "Ashigaru." "A Birdwatcher's Guide for Common Japanese Birds." *Japan Junky*, October 15, 2023. https://japanjunky.com/a-birdwatchers-guide-for-common-japanese-birds/.

Sundstrom, Bob. "Black Kites—Do Birds Start Fires?" *BirdNote* (podcast), January 6, 2022. https://www.birdnote.org/listen/shows/black-kites-do-birds-start-fires.

Sundstrom, Bob. "Grebes Like Their Meals with a Side of Feathers—Here's Why." *BirdNote* (podcast), January 25, 2021. https://www.audubon.org/news/grebes-their-meals-side-feathers-heres-why.

Wilke, Carolyn. "Like a Bird on a Wire That Starts a Wildfire." *New York Times*, June 29, 2022. https://www.nytimes.com/2022/06/29/science/birds-power-lines-wildfires.html.

WEBSITES

These are all excellent general references if you'd like to learn more about birds.

All About Birds, www.allaboutbirds.org

Audubon, www.audubon.org

Avibase, avibase.bsc-eoc.org

BirdLife Data Zone, datazone.birdlife.org

BirdLife International, www.birdlife.org

Birds of North America, www.birds-of-north-america.net

Birds of the World, birdsoftheworld.org

BTO | The British Trust for Ornithology, www.bto.org

Cornell Lab of Ornithology, www.birds.cornell.edu

Encyclopedia Britannica | Britannica, www.britannica.com

GBIF | Global Biodiversity Information Facility, www.gbif.org

Integrated Taxonomic Information System, www.itis.gov

Oiseaux-Birds, www.oiseaux-birds.com

RSPB | The Royal Society for the Protection of Birds, www.rspb.org.uk

Xeno-Canto—Bird Sounds from around the World, doi.org/10.15468/QV0KSN

Wikipedia, www.wikipedia.org

Acknowledgments

Writing a book is a solitary thing. Publishing one takes a village.

My sincere thanks to everyone at Chronicle Books who has been involved in bringing this book into the world. Special thanks to my editor, Steve Mockus, for helping me shape this book into something sharper and stronger than it was.

I owe a great debt of gratitude to my amazing agent, Ann Rittenberg, whose advocacy, advice, and friendship are dear to me. Her skill, experience, and delightfully fierce New York literary agent nature make her one of the best in the business, and exactly who a laid-back West Coast boy like me needs in his corner.

Thanks and gratitude to my family, who surround me with affection and support. I can't list you all here, but you know who you are. You make me laugh, you make me feel loved, and you keep me grounded. I am especially grateful to my wife and best friend, Gina, for her love, patience, and dogged encouragement.

Finally, I want to express my heartfelt thanks to all of my readers. You are the best. Your support makes it possible for me to continue doing what I love, and I hope that this and every book I ever write is worthy of the honor.

MORE DUMB BIRDS

The Field Guide to Dumb
Birds of North America

The Field Guide to Dumb Birds
of the Whole Stupid World

The Big Dumb
Bird Journal

The Field Guide to Dumb
Birds Sticker Book

SOME SMART BEES

OMFG, BEES!